BE
YOUR
OWN
ESTATE
AGENT

BE YOUR OWN ESTATE AGENT

Val Redding

BLANDFORD

Blandford Press
An imprint of Cassell, Artillery House, Artillery Row, London SW1P 1RT

First published 1989

Distributed in the United States by Sterling Publishing Co., Inc.,
2 Park Avenue, New York, NY 10016

Distributed in Australia by Capricorn Link (Australia) Pty Ltd,
PO Box 665, Lane Cove, NSW 2066

British Library Cataloguing in Publication Data

Redding, Val
   Be your own estate agent
   1. Residences. Sale, – Manuals – For owners
   I. Title
   333.33′8

ISBN 0-7137-2122-7

Typeset by St. George Typesetting, Redruth, Cornwall
Printed and bound in Great Britain by Courier International Ltd, Tiptree, Essex

Contents

Introduction

The purpose of this book is to provide a step-by-step selling guide for those people wishing to sell their homes without enlisting the help of a professional estate agent.

The reason why most people choose to sell their home themselves is, of course, to save estate agents' fees. As most agents charge commission, which can range from 1 to 3 per cent of the selling price, this can be a considerable amount of money. In addition to that, private sellers who plan their sale carefully, and understand exactly what they must do and why they must do it, will have the satisfaction of being in control of the situation from beginning to end. This in itself can take much of the worry and anxiety out of what can often be a very frustrating time.

The property world is in a constant state of change, so even if you have sold a property before *Be Your Own Estate Agent* will bring you right up to date and provide all the background information and technical data you need.

If you are selling your home, the chances are you will be buying another one at the same time, and you will be anxious to co-ordinate the two transactions. It is, therefore, essential that you find a buyer who can fall in line with your particular requirements and who is not likely to have problems raising enough money to complete the deal. You also need to sell your home for the highest possible price and to make sure you don't get involved in a never-ending chain of sales and purchases which might collapse altogether at the very last minute.

Although every sale is different, and every seller will undoubtedly have his or her own particular selling technique, the overall pattern of selling property is always similar. The same sort of problems arise and the same steps must be taken to overcome them. *Be Your Own Estate Agent* explains these steps and will help you to negotiate a satisfactory price for your property and to complete your transaction as quickly and efficiently as possible.

1.
ASSESSING THE SELLING PRICE

The first and most important thing to do before putting your home on the market is to find out the highest possible price you can ask for it. However, assessing its current market value is not as easy as it may seem, especially as there are so many factors which influence the value of property – not only *your* property, but the property market as a whole. The problem is that this is an area where you can't afford to make a mistake. If you price your home too high, you are unlikely to make a quick and efficient sale; too low and you will certainly lose money. In this chapter we will be considering the best ways of determining the right price to ask and looking in detail at the many factors which affect the price of property generally.

Comparisons

Probably the easiest way to find out the current market value of your home is to compare it with other properties which are similar to yours and situated in the same area, and set your basic price in line with these.

But before you come up with your final asking price, there are other factors to take into consideration too. For instance, you need to have a good idea of the amount of competition you face; that is, the amount of property for sale in your area, what type of property it is, and what price is being asked for it. Your local newspaper will provide much of the information you need. It is an easy enough task to read through the 'houses for sale' column, picking out descriptions of properties which sound the same as yours and are in the same location, and seeing what figures they are priced at. Visit your local estate agents too, and see what properties are being advertised in their windows. Are there any like yours? Is there a lot of property currently for sale in your

3

area? If you see a house similar in size and in the same general area as yours, what price is being asked for it?

Familiarise yourself with the current availability of property around you and the sort of prices being asked. Check out 'for sale' boards and 'sold' notices too. You need to get a 'feel' for the movement of property around you. Is there a lot being sold or are there lots of 'for sale' notices and very few 'sold' notices? If the latter is the case, it could mean that the property market as a whole is slow at the moment. Therefore, the price you come up with must be in line with other properties similar to yours in order to generate any interest at all. However, if there is very little for sale and what is for sale is obviously being sold fairly quickly, then you will be able to ask a higher price and, as long as it is within reason, you will probably get it.

It is this comparison of figures and turnover which you need to be aware of. If you over-price your property at a time when there are a lot of other homes for sale which are very similar to your own and in the same general area, you are unlikely to find a buyer quickly. On the other hand, you don't want to undervalue when there is little for sale and it is possible for you to ask a higher price than the norm.

There are other points to consider before you set the final marketing price on your home, so let us look at each of them in more detail.

How price is affected by area

If you divide any town or city into separate areas, you will find the price of property – even property which is almost the same in size and character – is just as divided. Certain roads or estates within an area will be more in demand than others, and it is surprising just how much influence this has on selling prices.

While trying to determine a good selling price, you must not overlook the fact that the area you live in will greatly affect the overall value of your home. For instance, a semi-detached, three-bedroomed house on a small development, with trees and parkland nearby, might command a much higher price than a similar semi-detached, three-bedroomed property which is one of an endless row of semi-detached houses in an area consisting of many other endless rows of similar property. Nevertheless, the two houses could well be presented to a high specification and offer exactly the same living-area and garden space.

It is, therefore, important for you to compare the prices of houses which are similar to your own and which are situated in the same area. If you only take into account the type of property and not the location, you could find yourself with completely the wrong market value for your particular home.

The whole country is similarly divided. Where there is employment, property prices boom. In depressed areas, where there are few jobs, prices stagnate, or even drop, and properties, when they are sold, go for prices well under their true value. It is a sad fact of life, but one you must not overlook if you are to come up with the right selling price for your home.

You will also notice that where public transport, especially train services, is easily accessible, the demand for property increases. People move away from busy town centres, where property prices are extremely high, and look for homes further away from their place of work – somewhere where there is an adequate means of transport to let them commute every day.

How demand will affect your price

The term 'a buyer's market' is used to describe the market when there are lots of properties for sale, with very few buyers to buy them. At times like these, buyers have a choice of property and sellers often find they must reduce their asking price in order to find any purchaser at all. Often, too, a property can remain on the market for a considerable length of time before a buyer is found. If you are selling during such a period, you must make sure that your property is presented at its very best in order to encourage viewers, that the asking price is not well above other properties which are the same as yours – or you certainly won't get anyone to view – and that you are prepared to negotiate the selling price in order to secure a sale.

The best course of action is to ask a price which is in line with others, but to make sure you have something special to offer the buyer. This could simply be that your home is presented in pristine decorative order, or perhaps you can offer a newly fitted kitchen, an extension, carpets and curtains, a larger than average plot – in fact any special feature that stands you apart from the rest. You will need to draw attention to yourself and offer just a little more than anyone else in order to draw one of those buyers who, after all, can pick and choose from many during such a period.

A 'seller's market' comes to the fore when there are lots of buyers ready and willing to buy, but there are very few properties available for them. Sellers then find buyers willing to pay the highest possible price in order to make a purchase. During such periods, considerable price increases are experienced, and sellers are tempted into 'gazumping' and 'contract race' situations as buyers try to outbid each other.

Therefore, the current level of demand for property is another influencing factor on property value. Where there is little demand, prices remain stagnant, but when demand is high, you can usually expect to get a good price for your property with little or no difficulty, as long as your price still remains realistic.

Seasonal changes

Surprisingly, demand for property fluctuates throughout the year, even in areas where property is in great demand. Spring is usually a busy time and ideal for those people selling property which is suitable for first-time buyers. Many young couples get married in the spring and are anxious to find a home to start them on the ladder of home-ownership. So this is a good time to sell if you have a starter home, or similar property in the price ranges suitable for first-time buyers.

Towards the end of the year, Christmas and New Year especially, the demand for property drops away, and you are more likely to find buyers moving home because they *have* to, rather than because they *want* to.

House buyers who simply want to move on to buy bigger and better property, and families who have outgrown their present home and need more living and bedroom space, tend not to move during the winter months unless they spot something very special. Consequently, family homes and more expensive or up-market properties usually sell more quickly at other times. Of course, this doesn't always apply, but if you put your property on the market at a quiet time of the year, you will certainly find the number of viewers dwindling away – although the viewers who do come will probably not be time-wasters.

As you can see, seasonal changes also affect the property market, and the time of year during which you put your home up for sale could affect the price. If you are anxious to sell very quickly – which could be the case if you are buying another home at the same time – you may have to drop the price a little during the quieter times of year, but if you can afford to wait until the market moves on again, it should not affect the price.

The money market

Over recent years building societies and banks have lent more and more money to home-buyers, and they have been in a position to meet the demand for higher mortgages as property prices continue to increase.

With this has come the introduction of different mortgage packages, different multiples of salary and all sorts of investment accounts designed to encourage people to save and to provide them with a basis on which to borrow money when they want to buy a home. As house prices continue to rise, so it has become more and more difficult for first-time buyers to afford to buy anything at all, but, here again, lenders have come up with various packages to help them over this initial very high hurdle.

All this has been good news for sellers, as it has allowed the market to be funded generally. Hopefully, it is a trend which will continue. However, there are still times when lenders do not have as much money as they need to meet every application as it is received, and long queues of potential borrowers begin to form.

When lenders are able to meet the demand for mortgages, and multiples of salary are fairly high, then there are usually a good number of buyers about, because more people find themselves able to obtain advances allowing them to purchase a property that might otherwise be beyond their means. The situation is somewhat different, however, when mortgage funds are limited and lenders have only a certain amount of money to lend per month. At these times, if an application is received after that amount has been allocated, the application must move to the end of the queue and will be considered when more funds are available. In such circumstances, a borrower may find he or she has to wait several months before their advance is forthcoming. If you put your property on the market during a period when funds are limited, you will need to choose your purchaser with the greatest of care (more details in Chapter 7).

Lack of mortgage funds often brings about a stagnant period in the property market: there is plenty of property for sale, but few people in a position to buy. This can also happen when there is a sudden rise in mortgage interest rates and buyers become more cautious about the amount they borrow. As we have already mentioned, during such a period you must make sure the price at which you market your property is competitive or you will be unlikely to net one of the few buyers who *is* able to raise a mortgage and complete the purchase.

How terms of leases affect the price

The value of leasehold property can be greatly affected by the number of years remaining on the lease.

Check the terms and conditions of your lease – you will need much of the information later on anyway – and find out how many years are outstanding.

Some lenders restrict their lending on leasehold properties where less than 50 or 55 years remain on the lease and this will greatly affect the saleability and value of your home. What it means is that anyone needing to borrow a high proportion of the selling price, by way of a mortgage, may find the lender unwilling to advance the full amount required, or unwilling to allow the term of the advance to run for the maximum number of years. This in turn will limit the number of people in a position to buy your home, as some may not be able to obtain the finance they need to complete the deal.

This applies especially to flat-owners. If you own a leasehold house, the Leasehold Reform Act 1967 gives leaseholders the right to buy their freehold. You may not have taken up this option, but your purchaser may wish to do so, which will make the selling of your leasehold house that much easier. It is certainly worth checking with your solicitor to find out all the details, including the terms and conditions under which the Act applies, and if the right to buy can be transferred to your buyer in the event of a sale.

Listed buildings and conservation areas

If you own a listed building or live within a conservation area, then you will be aware that such a building and/or area has been listed as being of special interest to the public and must not be altered or extended in any way without prior consent from the local authority.

If you have undertaken repairs of any kind, for which planning consent was required, make available all the documentation for your prospective buyer to inspect. This also applies if you have obtained planning consent for work which has not yet been carried out. Your buyer will need to satisfy himself that any building work undertaken, or to be undertaken, has received the appropriate consent and that he is not about to enter into negotiations to purchase a listed property which has been altered in such a way that it is in breach of any legislation which might apply. If your listed home is of historical or architectural interest, it will be included in the quarterly publication of listed buildings produced by the Historic Buildings Bureau of the Department of the Environment (see Useful addresses). You might like to get a copy to present to your buyer.

If a listed building falls below a certain standard, it may be eligible for a grant (available from your local authority), especially if essential structural repairs are required. Grants are also available for any other property which does not have certain basic facilities, such as a bath or shower, lavatory, hot and cold water supply, basin or sink. Any grant will be dependent upon what the local authority terms as an 'eligible expense', and the amount of the grant will be a percentage of that amount. Details are contained in the brochure 'Home Improvement Grants, a guide for home-owners, landlords and tenants' which is available from your local authority free of charge. Grants are usually higher for property in Greater London than elsewhere. If your property might be eligible for such a grant, it is worth making a few inquiries at this stage so that the relevant information can be passed on to prospective buyers. If they are aware that financial help could be forthcoming to bring the property up to standard, it could possibly sway them into buying.

Listed property is often sought-after by buyers looking for something just a little bit special. Consequently, you may find it difficult to set a price on your home in view of the fact that it is probably a 'one-off' and comparisons are therefore almost impossible.

This will apply, of course, to any property which has an individual character, and it may be necessary in this situation to enlist the help of a professional valuer to establish an accurate marketing price for your home. Most estate agents will carry out a valuation free of charge, although they may make a small charge if you let it be known that you intend to sell privately. There may also be a charge for a valuation undertaken by a surveyor. At this stage, however, a market valuation by an estate agent is all you really need, and he will probably carry it out for you free of charge, even if very reluctantly!

Part-exchange

Many developers now offer schemes designed to encourage buyers to complete the purchase of their new homes as quickly as possible. Often included is a part-exchange scheme.

You may have decided to participate in such a scheme if only to avoid the problems associated with selling a property yourself. What you must remember, however, is that the developer is only likely to offer you up to 95 per cent of the current market value of your home, although the subsequent legal costs you will incur could be reduced.

The developer will ask a local valuer to put a price on your property and will then offer you the agreed percentage of that figure. If this is acceptable to you, the deal will go through, leaving you free to complete the purchase of your new home. Your old property will then be put up for sale by the developer in the usual way.

This is all very well, but you must consider whether or not you could do better if you were to sell your home yourself. Find out all the facts and figures about the deal and then decide if you would be in a better financial position if you did not participate in the part-exchange. If the property market as a whole is progressive and buoyant, then the chances are you will still be able to sell successfully, and complete your purchase according to plan.

Special features

A property which has been extended, modernised or is in excellent decorative order both inside and out will certainly command the highest price within its own level of similar properties. However, bear in mind that some alterations, such as double glazing and large extensions do not always give a good return on your outlay unless your property is of an individual nature and/or in a non-estate position.

A two-bedroomed property extended to three or more bedrooms, or the addition of a garage and/or central heating, will certainly reap its full reward. Unfortunately, there are still people who overspend on their property, which is all very well if you intend to stay in the house until prices generally increase to meet your outlay, but not altogether helpful if you sell soon after the alterations have been completed. What can happen here is that the value of your house is increased, but prices it out of the market in comparison with other property in the area. What you need to consider is whether a purchaser will pay an exceedingly high price for your property when he or she might be able to purchase a similar home just down the road, but without all the alterations and for less money. The secret is to keep your price within the level appropriate to your type of home in your particular area. If you overprice, you will certainly have problems selling.

Fixtures and fittings

Many people leave fitted carpets and other items, such as light fittings, curtains and other fixtures, in their home when they move. These often attract more buyers, especially as they are such expensive items to install when you first move in.

On the other hand, the surveyor who values your home when the buyer applies for his or her mortgage is primarily concerned with the value of the building itself and will not take too much notice of the second-hand items left in it.

In deciding on the right marketing price, it is important to aim your figure at the *building*. By all means leave things like carpets and curtains if you want to, especially as it will encourage more enquiries, but if you want extra money for these, make an itemised list and state quite clearly how much you want for each. Your buyer can then decide what, if anything, he or she wants to buy and you can negotiate an acceptable figure.

If you intend to leave certain fixtures and fittings anyway, then make this clear to viewers, but remember you are, in effect, including them 'free of charge' within the asking price of the property.

The sale of fixtures and fittings can prove something of a headache if they are not dealt with properly right from the word go, so make sure you know what you are leaving and what you are selling separately. When you show people around the house, point out these things so that there can be no doubt. Whatever you do, when you move out, *never* take anything you originally agreed to leave behind.

If you are not sure what a fixture or fitting actually is, apply the criteria that if when removing the item you damage the property itself, then it should not be removed at all and is part of the dwelling anyway!

Unfortunately, however, this is something of a grey area and open to argument, so in the long run, the most satisfactory solution is to make up a list to discuss with your buyer. Your buyer's solicitor will eventually ask for this information anyway.

Age and condition

Of course, another important influence on price is the age and condition of your home. As we have already mentioned, if the property falls below a certain standard, then it could be eligible for a grant towards the improvements necessary. This could help you sell, especially as there will always be buyers on the look-out for homes to refurbish and modernise. On the other hand, a property, however old, sold in good condition will always command a good price.

Calculating your final figure

At this point youshould be in a position to set a realistic marketing price on your home. Remember to allow an amount for negotiation, but in doing so don't price yourself out of the market as a whole.

Don't round off thousands either – go down! For instance, a figure of £64,950 is far more appealing than a figure of £65,000. It will attract buyers who don't think they can afford £65,000 and who would not bother to contact you if you advertised at the higher figure.

It is also important to calculate the lowest figure you could possibly accept, taking into account all your own expenses and costs. Keep this figure in mind and if you have to accept reduced offers on your sale, make sure you don't drop below that figure and perhaps find yourself in financial difficulties later on. The object of the exercise is to make a profit on your sale and to achieve the highest possible price for your property which also takes into account the expenses and costs of your move.

Conclusion

In this chapter we have discussed all the factors which are likely to influence the market value of your home. Let's look again at the important points to remember:

- Don't think your house is worth far more than anyone else's just because *you* live there

- Your final asking price must be realistic

- Allow a little extra for negotiation, but not enough to price your property out of competition with similar homes.

- Set yourself an asking price *and* the lowest figure you can afford to accept

- Remember that if you *over-price* you are going to have a problem selling

- If you *under-price*, the loss is yours!

- If you over-price and don't sell, you can still reduce the price

13

and try again.

- If you under-price and then realise your error, it will be very difficult to put up the price and still find a buyer. Potential buyers notice these things and are not usually very impressed!

- Don't round off thousands, go down

- If you can't come up with the right price on your own, ask an estate agent for a free valuation.

Remember too that your buyer will probably require a mortgage and his or her lender will expect the property to offer good security for the amount of money required, so from that point of view alone, an accurate assessment of value is essential.

In any event, a property is only worth what someone is willing to pay for it and most buyers know exactly what they want for their money. As a final test, put yourself in the position of a prospective buyer and decide if you would pay that amount of money for that type of property, and if not, why not?

2.
WHAT THE BUYER
WILL LOOK FOR

There are many things prospective buyers look for in a property and it is almost impossible to predict every one. There are all sorts of questions you are likely to be asked too, and it is important for the seller always to offer constructive and positive answers. In this chapter we will be discussing some of the formal elements of house-ownership which you are unlikely to have to recite off by heart, but which you should understand fully in order to give clear and concise answers to any questions that might crop up. You will want to negotiate a sale which will complete and not fall through just when you think everything is progressing well, so careful preparation and a little initial groundwork is better done at this stage, in order to give a clear picture of exactly what your house has to offer, rather than leave a prospective buyer wondering if he or she has in fact made the right decision to buy. These are the buyers that nearly always change their minds later.

Presentation

The first thing that any buyer will look for is the way your home is presented.

Don't give buyers an excuse to offer you a low price by putting the house on the market in a shoddy and untidy condition. That does not mean the whole building should be completely redecorated and refurnished! It simply means that it should be clean and tidy and that all essential maintenance is undertaken. Don't assume that it doesn't really matter – in such a competitive field as the housing market it most certainly does!

All too often sellers complain that viewers stop outside their home and then drive on again without even coming in, and it must be said that many people do judge the book only by its cover! So start by taking a good look at the outside of your home. Tidy the garden, mend the gate and, if necessary, wipe over or touch up outside paintwork. Even the smallest entrance can be greatly enhanced with hanging baskets or tubs of flowers. Make your home look inviting and always remember that first impressions count, and the first impression buyers will have of your home will be of the outside.

If you need to redecorate rooms, now is the time to do it. But make it simple: not everyone likes bold stripes or bunches of flowers on their wallpaper. Neither does everyone enjoy bright green walls or yellow paintwork. Keep colour schemes gentle and, wherever possible, carefully co-ordinated. Bear in mind that whatever décor you choose, the new buyer will probably redecorate anyway.

Even more important than décor is cleanliness. A greasy kitchen stacked high with dirty washing-up and smelling of yesterday's dinner is not going to do much to help you sell. Bathrooms too must always be clean – it doesn't take much effort but it does make a difference. Don't clutter rooms either, especially small rooms.

Of course, you may have a property which needs a great deal of maintenance and refurbishment. If it is eligible for a grant (see section on Listed buildings and conservation areas in Chapter 1), this will provide a starting-point on which to base your negotiations, especially if you have no intention of tackling the work yourself prior to the sale. If this is the case, you must make sure your asking price takes into account the amount of work which is outstanding. Be prepared for some hard haggling over the price too. As we have already mentioned, all buyers are looking for a bargain, and many people are on the look-out for property which they can 'do-up' and sell again. Such buyers will always haggle – and if they require a mortgage, the condition of your property will play an important part with regard to the amount they are able to borrow.

Where you are selling in competition with several similar properties, presenting your home at its very best is essential. A homely and welcoming atmosphere is always pleasant. A few flowers, scented soap in the bathroom – it all helps to create an inviting atmosphere and it is the *feel* of a house which often finally persuades the viewer to buy.

Location

Viewers will want to know about the area in general too. Families with children will need to know where the nearest schools, play groups and further education colleges are situated. Most importantly, they will want to know how their children can get there, so find out as much as you can about school bus routes and be in a position to answer any questions that might come up about local education.

Familiarise yourself with the availability of your local public transport services and, if possible, arm yourself with a copy of timetables.

Everyone needs a doctor or a dentist at some time or another, so be prepared to give information about their whereabouts in relation to your house and details about the nearest hospital services.

Many families will have elderly relatives to care for and you could well be asked about special facilities for older people, such as clubs and day centres.

Where is the nearest shopping centre? Is there a regular bus service to and from it? What about the nearest church? Which denomination does it represent? What about social activities, pubs, clubs, cinema, theatre?

You may consider all this irrelevant, but for newcomers to your area it is essential information that an efficient estate agent would certainly be in a position to provide, so be prepared and don't lose the interest of a prospective buyer just because you can't be bothered. You can't afford to present an inattentive or negative attitude when you are trying to sell a house, and the 'sorry, I don't know' reply projects just that attitude.

Running costs of the property

The vast majority of people purchase the most expensive property they can afford. It is, therefore, essential that they organise their finances carefully. It follows that they must take into account how much the property is likely to cost them to run once they have moved in.

Most lenders will need to know the rateable value of a property.

Your buyer will have to include these details on his or her mortgage application form, so make sure you know the rateable value of your home, including the water rates, and the amount payable. If you are not sure, then check it out with your local rates office. A telephone call is all you need to make. The proposed 'poll tax' will, of course, affect such figures if and when it comes into effect.

The running cost of your central-heating system is another point that most viewers want to discuss. Keep a copy of your latest bill for reference, so that you are able to give some idea of annual charges. If you have oil-fired central heating, indicate how much oil is currently stored and is likely to be left when the property is finally sold.

The question of gas and electricity costs is likely to come up too. If the property is leasehold, make sure you have the following details available:

- Number of years left on the lease
- Ground rent payable per annum
- Maintenance charges and what they are for:
  −maintenance of shared driveways and forecourts
  −upkeep of stairs and hallways
  −general upkeep of other communal areas and facilities
- Insurance premiums. You will have been responsible for paying a proportion of the insurance of the whole building which covers such things as fire or other damage to the whole building, rather than just to your portion of it. Arm yourself with a copy of the lease and insurance documents and be prepared to explain to the purchaser what exactly is covered by the insurance. It is important that he or she fully understands what cover they are going to be responsible for, and at what point the freeholder's responsibilities take over.
- Any other charges which apply to the property:
  −a charge for a porter or security guard
  −a charge for renting a garage if one is not included with the property
  −a charge for any shared hot water or heating system

There is a selection of questions which the sellers of leasehold flats and maisonettes may well be asked, including:

- Which garage belongs to the property?
- If there is no garage, what parking space is available?

- Where is there parking space for visitors?
- Does the landlord carry out his responsibilities properly?
- Are there any shared gardens or facilities to which rules and regulations apply and if so, what are they?
- Are there any restrictions which apply, such as not hanging out washing at certain times?
- Are the neighbours quiet or do you hear much noise from adjoining flats?

Full details of both the terms and conditions of the lease and the insurance cover is a matter for the buyer's solicitor to look into fully before contracts are drawn up, and the buyer may not think to ask you many of these questions when he first comes to view. Nevertheless, it is a good idea to have the information handy – remember, always give positive answers to all questions if you want to make a sale!

Your buyer may be interested to know that the local department of the environment provides a free leaflet entitled 'Service Charge in Flats'. This sets out the occupiers' rights under the Housing Act 1980.

Covenants

There are certain activities which an owner of a property may or may not carry out on the property or its land. These are called covenants. A restrictive covenant is something which the owner must not do. A positive covenant is something which he or she must do. For instance, you may not be allowed to store a caravan or a boat in the garden. You may not be allowed to keep livestock in the garden, dogs or cats in blocks of flats, or you may be prohibited from planting trees in the front garden in case it obscures the view of the road and therefore becomes a safety hazard for traffic.

Other restrictive covenants could prevent you from running a business from the property or putting up other buildings on the land.

Then there are those activities which the owner may be obliged to undertake, such as maintaining the boundary fence or wall to a certain standard, or maintaining the appearance of the property and its land to a prescribed standard.

Preservation orders on trees or certain hedgerows adjoining or on the premises may also apply, and the owner may not be able to fell or lop the trees without special permission.

These are all matters which the buyer's solicitor must investigate, but again, prospective buyers may be looking out for these things too, so be prepared.

Guarantees

If you have had double glazing installed, cavity-wall insulation, rewiring or perhaps special timber treatment undertaken, for which guarantees still apply, do make sure you make this clear.

Buyers will be expecting some sort of assurance that the work was carried out properly, especially as things like timber treatment and similar work are so expensive. They may also expect assurance that the work was undertaken by a professional rather than a DIY enthusiast. Their solicitor, too, may ask for evidence that guarantees exist.

If you are a DIY buff and any work you have completed is to a good standard, then there is unlikely to be a problem. But, unfortunately, not all do-it-yourselfers do it well, and we then have to face the problems which are inevitably spotted by the buyer's surveyor.

If you are including built-in appliances in the price, such as ovens, hobs, washing-machines and so on, make sure that each appliance is in good working order and that ovens and hobs are clean and well-presented. Guarantees and manufacturers' instruction manuals should be made available too.

Conclusion

Different people look for different things when they buy property. Everyone sets his or her own value on certain aspects of a home. A busy housewife, for instance, will be looking at the kitchen and what facilities it offers, while a keen gardener may put the size and nature of the overall plot as a priority.

As a seller, you can never really tell what the viewer is looking for, so it is most important that you prepare yourself properly before you start to market your home, and make sure you are in a position to respond to any sort of question which could come up.

Of course, you are unlikely to be asked 'what covenants apply?' or 'what are the terms and conditions of the lease?', but your viewers may well ask if they can keep a caravan in the front garden or chickens in the back. In a block of flats, they may want to know who it is that paints and maintains the communal hallway and stairs, or what happens if a fire in an adjoining flat damages his.

If you understand the legal implications of such questions, you will be in a better position to put forward constructive answers.

Some people may argue that all this preparation is quite unnecessary, but if you expect your sale to complete in the quickest possible time, and with the minimum of problems, you must be properly prepared.

Sorting out all this information at a point later in the proceedings could well cause a great deal of delay and may even provoke the buyer into withdrawing from the deal altogether. If a long chain of sales and purchases is involved, such a delay might just tip the scales enough to cause the whole chain to collapse, and you will have to start all over again.

3.
HOW MORTGAGES WILL AFFECT YOUR BUYER

You may think that the mortgage your buyer will be getting has nothing to do with you and will have no bearing on the way in which you conduct the negotiations for your sale. Well, you are wrong.

There are many aspects of a mortgage application which affect the buyer's ability to purchase the property and could well make a great difference to your chances of selling. In this chapter we will be looking at different types of mortgages and discussing which elements could affect the saleability of your home and which elements you must take into account when determining whether or not your prospective buyer is a 'good bet' and likely to be able to complete the deal without any problems. For information purposes, other details about mortgages have also been included, which might be useful to you if you are applying for a loan yourself.

The availability of funds

In Chapter 1 we looked at the way the price of property can be affected by the availability of mortgage funds, and as we discussed, at times when there is a shortage of money for house buying, long queues of borrowers begin to form, each waiting their turn for the next available issue of money.

Fortunately, many lenders now issue applicants with written confirmation that a mortgage has been agreed *in principle* and that funds have been allocated, subject to survey. If your buyer can produce this evidence, then you can be pretty sure he or she will not have a problem raising the purchase money, as long as the surveyor for the lender doesn't turn up anything horrendous when your home is surveyed. If you sell when there is little money around, and especially if you are anxious to complete another purchase very quickly, don't sell to anyone who can't offer you some assurance that he or she can raise the purchase money in time.

Another point to bear in mind is that most estate agents are able to offer their clients special mortgage facilities. Recent legislation has allowed banks, building societies and insurance companies to move into the field of house sales and many now own chains of estate agents offering their financial services. Competition between these bodies is fierce and at the time of writing (late 1988) it is not difficult for applicants to raise money for their purchase. In fact, much concern is being voiced because many buyers are tempted into borrowing more money than they can easily afford to pay back. This often results in the borrower finding himself in financial difficulties later on, and in a growing number of cases, not being able to repay the loan, forcing the lender to repossess the property and leaving the borrower homeless. As you can see, the temptations are great, so if you are getting a mortgage yourself, don't borrow more than you can reasonably afford to pay back. Take into account any changes in your life-style that may affect your status in the future, especially where two salaries are taken into account when the loan is first made and one of those salaries may not be permanent, perhaps because a wife leaves work to start a family.

As a private seller, you do not have the advantage of being able to offer your buyer mortgage facilities, and your buyer must approach a lender direct for his loan. If the buyer has done his or her homework well, this should not be a problem. From your point of view, however, you must make sure your prospective buyer is not stringing you along. It's no good agreeing to sell to someone who has absolutely no idea how much he can borrow and is simply 'hoping' he can get the amount he wants as soon as he wants it. Such a buyer is most unlikely to complete the deal.

Restrictions on advances

Some lenders set down rules and regulations about the type of property on which they will advance a high percentage of the purchase price by way of a mortgage.

Usually, a person, whose financial status is secure, can borrow the maximum percentage of purchase price allowed. This is 75 or 80 per cent of the *valuation* figure the lender puts on the property. If the borrower requires a higher percentage, additional security is required by the lender. This usually takes the form of a mortgage-guarantee bond, or indemnity policy which the lender arranges through an insurance company and for which the borrower must pay one single premium.

As a seller, it is worth remembering that it is 75 or 80 per cent of the sum of money the lender's surveyor considers the property to be worth – *the valuation figure* – and not necessarily your asking price. So if you have a buyer who needs a high mortgage, and your home is down-valued by the lender, you will have another problem to overcome (see Chapter 10).

In some cases, lenders consider certain types of property to be less appropriate for a high percentage advance than others. They may restrict the percentage of valuation on these properties, which include:

- Flats which are above a certain floor level
- Flats which have been converted and were not purpose built as flats (although this ruling is sometimes waived in London where many flats have been converted)
- Property below a certain standard (i.e. without an inside toilet, a bathroom or hot-water system)
- A leasehold property with less than a certain number of years remaining on the lease
- Property which is not of a conventional structure (i.e. brick built)
- A property with a sitting tenant.

These restrictions differ from lender to lender, but, nevertheless, as a seller you should be aware that they exist. Let us say, for instance, that you have a house to sell where there is a sitting tenant and a first-time buyer comes along who needs a 95 per cent mortgage. You must appreciate that he could have a problem raising that sort of money on your home if his lender applies restrictions to loans on properties with sitting tenants. You need, here, to keep your home on the market and tell the first-time buyer that you are not prepared to close the deal unless he has a firm mortgage offer.

As you can see, if you are aware of potential problem areas, you can deal with them effectively right from the word go, and you are less likely to be drawn into negotiations which eventually fall through.

Different mortgage packages

Let us look now at some of the various mortgage packages which are currently available. They will not affect you as the seller of a property, but you may certainly find the information handy if you are taking out a mortgage yourself.

Repayment or annuity mortgage

This type of loan works in much the same way as an ordinary hire-purchase agreement. You borrow a lump sum over an agreed period and each month you pay back a little of the capital and the appropriate interest. As the years progress, the amount you owe decreases until at the end of the term the capital is repaid in full. You will need a mortgage-protection insurance to accompany this type of loan, so that if you die the amount outstanding will be repaid and your heirs will not find themselves with a heavy debt to pay.

Endowment

This type of loan differs from the above in as much as the amount of the loan remains outstanding throughout the term of the loan.

The monthly repayments consist of interest and the premium due on the endowment policy which is an integral part of the package. At the end of the term, the policy matures to pay off the capital in full. If the package is *with profit*, there will probably be a lump-sum payment made to you as well. Where a *non-profit* endowment mortgage has been arranged, the policy, when it matures, will provide enough money to pay off the capital, but there will not be a payment of bonuses to the borrower. The policy itself provides cover for the loan to be repaid if the borrower should die before the end of the term.

Low start mortgage

A package for first-time buyers where at the beginning of the term, usually for the first five years or so, premiums and repayments are kept to a minimum. After that initial period, however, they are increased. This package is aimed at first-time buyers who are at the beginning of their career and whose prospects for advancement and salary increases are good, as it is assumed that their salary will have increased sufficiently to meet the higher repayments when they become due and the financial advantage gained by the lower repayments at the beginning of the term are received when they are most needed.

Pension mortgage

This package is aimed at the self-employed person, or someone who does not belong to a company pension scheme of any kind. It is linked to an insurance policy and interest is paid monthly throughout the term of the advance. The capital is repaid on retirement, when the policy matures, and it also provides a pension. Tax relief is available on the pension premiums and the cost of the life cover. You need to make sure, however, that the pension provided is going to be adequate for your needs in retirement.

Other packages are available and it is worth shopping around to compare the terms and conditions offered by various lenders before you decide which is most suitable for you.

Terms of loans

The number of years over which a mortgage can be borrowed is a matter of choice. The maximum number of years usually offered is 25, although some lenders will extend this term. It is sensible to organise yourself so that your mortgage will be paid off on or before you retire. In any event, your loan must be repaid in full when you sell your house. You will then have to apply for another advance to purchase again. If you have an endowment policy, however, the endowment itself can be transferred to another property and adjusted to meet any change in your needs at that time.

Buyers and their status

There should be no cause for concern if your buyer is a self-employed person, as long as he has been self-employed for some time. Lenders will expect him to produce audited accounts to prove his income before they will offer him a loan, but if you are in any doubt as to his purchasing capability, keep your home on the market until he can confirm that he has arranged a suitable mortgage.

A single woman buying a home will be treated in the same way as a working man. She must provide adequate income and secure employment just the same as anyone else.

Where a property is being purchased jointly, the income of each of the buyers will go towards the advance, but as from August 1988 only one claim per property can be made for tax relief.

First time buyers

Selling to a first-time buyer who has arranged a mortgage, in principle, will undoubtedly make your life a great deal easier. You will not have the worry of being drawn into a long chain of sales and purchases, except, of course, any beyond your own new purchase. You will also have a good indication that your buyer is not likely to hold up the proceedings while he or she chases around trying to raise the money.

Tax relief

Borrowers are entitled to tax relief on the interest they pay on mortgages up to £30,000. This relief is usually deducted from the monthly repayments by the lender under the MIRAS scheme – Mortgage Interest Relief at Source. The most common form in which the scheme is applied is the level-term MIRAS, where the repayments remain constant over the life of the mortgage. Gross-profile MIRAS is an alternative adopted by some lenders. Here the relief is adjusted with each payment, so that maximum relief is allowed at the beginning of the term, decreasing in relation to repayments as the term advances. Gross-profile MIRAS can be helpful for the first-time buyer who needs every penny when he or she first purchases a home.

Interest rates

Interest rates fluctuate and can differ from lender to lender. If you are looking for a mortgage yourself, shop around for the best deal and note that lenders sometimes change interest rates on advances above certain levels. Even during the term of the advance, interest rates may fluctuate. If you take out a repayment mortgage and the rate goes up, you are usually given the opportunity to extend the term of the advance or to uplift your repayments in line with the increase. It is certainly worth meeting the increase if you can, or the term could be extended indefinitely.

However, an endowment mortgage is different. Here any increase must be met by the borrower so that the loan runs concurrently with the policy.

Conclusion

It is fair to say that many chains of sales and purchases fall through because somewhere someone has a problem at the mortgage stage. It is, therefore, very important that you avoid arranging a sale to someone who might have a problem raising the money. The secret is to be prepared. Be aware of the many factors which govern the mortgageability of property and the problems which borrowers have to face when they apply for loans. In Chapter 7 we will be looking more closely at the questions you need to ask a prospective buyer in order to establish whether or not he or she is in a good position to arrange finance and to make sure they are not likely to let you down at the last minute.

Remember, too, that the onus is on you to make sure your home is good security for a mortgage. That is to say, that it is not over-priced in relation to its age, condition and what it has to offer, to the extent that a surveyor will not consider it to be sound security for an advance, and therefore 'down-value' it. Remember that the lender will base his advance on the valuation figure the surveyor comes up with, which might not be as much as the agreed selling price. Such is the importance of marketing your home at the right price as we discussed in Chapter 1.

In the last three chapters, we have looked at the background and preparation to selling property. Now let us put our property on the market and use this knowledge to negotiate a successful sale.

4.
ADVERTISING
YOUR HOME

Advertising outlets

Having decided on a realistic figure to ask for your home, and armed with all the background information we have already discussed, the next step is to sort out how and where you are going to advertise.

Your first choice will probably be your local newspaper, and don't forget that in many areas there are a number of free newspapers circulated on a regular basis, too. But although they are free to the consumer, there is, of course, a charge for advertising in them. Find out how much they charge and bear in mind that many papers offer reduced rates if you place the same advertisement more than once.

Charges will be based on the type of advertisement you choose to place. Start by scrutinising the way houses are advertised already and pick out the type of advertisement which you consider to be the most eye-catching. Obviously it is more expensive to advertise with an accompanying photograph, but most readers looking for a property to buy look at the photographs first, and as you are advertising just one property, then you must make sure readers can spot your advertisement easily. So if your property is attractive from the outside, include a photograph with your advertisement.

A full display advertisement is going to be the most expensive, but there is also the classified section with smaller semi-displays and line advertisements. If you want to make an impact, choose the most expensive one you can afford. Remember you will be competing with estate agents who are in a position to place full-page advertisements. You need to *get yourself noticed*.

There are other outlets, too. Try placing a postcard, with a photograph, in local store windows. If you live near large national companies, why not let their personnel departments know you have a house for sale? You never know, they may be looking for property for new staff moving into the area. There are also a number of monthly magazines currently being published which advertise houses for sale. They are not cheap to advertise in, but nevertheless worth considering. Some also specialise, for example, in cottages and country properties.

If you are very lucky, you may find a buyer from your very first advertisement. Unfortunately, selling houses is rarely that easy and you will probably need to run your advertisement for at least a couple of weeks.

Another avenue of approach is to start with a simple classified advertisement, and if you get no response at all, try again with a bigger and better display. In any event, if you don't get any replies to your advertisement, it is probably because the advertisement is inadequate or the home's price is wrong. If you run the advertisement several times and change the wording and layout each time, but still get no replies, it's a sure sign that the problem lies with the price, especially at times when the market is in full swing and demand is high. So look again at your asking price and, if appropriate, lower it a little. Sometimes, even a slight reduction in price can make the difference between receiving no enquiries at all, and receiving too many to deal with all at once.

For Sale signs

There is no reason why you should not make up a For Sale sign and place it in your garden. Make sure it is secure, though, and not likely to clout someone on the head if it falls down when the wind catches it. You also need to check with your local authority that it is not in breach of any local restrictions on the erection of boards.

A window poster is another source of advertising, but if you are to avoid people hammering on your door just as you get into the bath, make it clear on both boards and poster that viewing is *Strictly by Appointment* and give a telephone number where you can be contacted. If you are at work all day, make sure you also give a daytime number. Sales can be lost just because vendors cannot be contacted – as a private seller you can't afford to take that chance. If you are quite happy to have callers at all times of the day and night, then you can state *Apply Within*. Regrettably, this often encourages 'Nosy Parkers' who have no intention of buying anything at all – and they are the ones who arrive just as you get in the bath!

Make your board up carefully and ensure it says *House* or *Flat For Sale*. If you just say For Sale, then you could be selling just about anything. Your board should be well presented. A piece of cardboard nailed to a stick is not likely to encourage enquiries – people will assume the inside of your home is just as shoddy.

A board or window poster is certainly worth considering if you want to catch the attention of the many buyers who tour the area they want to live in in their cars at evenings and weekends. It is an advertising medium not to be overlooked.

Preparing your advertisement

The most important thing to do in any advertisement is to point out the best and most outstanding features of what you have to sell. You may well be advertising a home which is exactly the same as the house next door, which is also for sale. Even the price could be the same, so if you are to attract buyers, you must find some way of convincing them that your house is the better buy.

You also need to arrange your advertisement so that the points which most interest the readers are the ones which come first. Failure to do that and they may read no further.

Here again, look closely at the advertisements in your local paper. Pick out any that you consider to be outstanding and circle them. Use them as a guide for your own advertisement.

Try to avoid jargon. Estate agents use it all the time, but it looks silly if private sellers try and incorporate it in their advertisements. Be clear and concise and *never* mislead the reader.

The following are examples of good advertising practice and can be used with a photograph in a full display or in the classified section:

SOUTHAMPTON – £44,950. 2-bedroomed semidetached house suitable for first-time buyers. Fitted kitchen, open lounge/dining-room, bath/shower room, gas central heating garage and garden. Tel. Southampton 12345.

Notice that here we have made a special mention of the open lounge/dining-room and that the bathroom also has a shower. We have also addressed our advertisement to the sort of buyer who would most likely be looking for a property such as this.

> **ROMSEY OUTSKIRTS** – Detached bungalow with large
> secluded garden. 3 bedrooms, lounge, fitted kitchen, bath-
> room, separate WC, oil-fired central heating, garage, work-
> shop. £78,500 to include carpets and curtains. Telephone.
> Romsey 123456.

Here we have placed the emphasis on the large garden and made it
clear that it is not in the heart of the town. We will assume that
this particular bungalow has no other special features we could have
mentioned, but we are including carpets and curtains in the sale to
encourage enquiries.

> **MARINA VILLAGE** – Executive-styled, 5-bedroomed resi-
> dence with mooring, elevated lounge with balcony over-
> looking harbour, dining-room with terrace, *en suite* shower
> room, 2 further bathrooms, study, fully fitted kitchen with
> built-in appliances, utility room, double garage, patio garden,
> £555,995 leasehold. Telephone Hythe 123456.

This type of property is best advertised with an accompanying
photograph. If you have a special or individual property, then you
should certainly consider advertising in one of the specialist magazines
which are currently available.

> **TOTTON** – **£75,550 Freehold.** Detached house, built 1975,
> situated in quiet cul-de-sac. Master bedroom with fitted
> wardrobes and *en suite* shower room, 3 further bedrooms
> (2 double, 1 single) each with built-in wardrobes, family
> bathroom, cloakroom, large lounge with feature brick fire-
> place, luxury fitted kitchen with breakfast bar and range
> of fitted appliances, separate dining-room with patio doors
> opening into recently erected sun room, double glazing
> throughout, full gas-fired central heating, garage, secluded
> landscaped garden. Carpets and matching Austrian blinds
> can be purchased by separate arrangement. Telephone
> Totton 654321 evenings and weekends, or Southampton
> 123456 during office hours.

Here we have an advertisement which gives far more detail than
some of the others. It also indicates that the family are working
and includes alternative telephone numbers. It describes some of the
special features of the property (for example, the brick fireplace) and
gives an example for an advertisement for a property which might

be one of several others currently for sale in the same location and around the same price. If the property next door was being advertised as follows, which of the two advertisements would you consider the most effective and would probably get the most replies — the one below, or the previous one?

> **4-bedroomed house, Totton,** bathroom, *en suite*, kitchen, dining-room, lounge, double glazing and central heating, garden, some extras, £75,550 Tel. Totton 123456.

If your home is attractive to look at, then advertise with a photograph if you can possibly afford it. Make sure you include the general location of the property and the price, and don't forget a telephone number. You may decide to use a box number, but this often puts prospective buyers off, as they seem to think you have something to hide, and they rarely bother to reply. Don't advertise without a price either. Buyers get very suspicious and usually come to the conclusion that you are frightened to include it because you're asking too much anyway!

Write out two or three different versions of your advertisement before you decide on the final one. Usually the paper will abbreviate certain words for you. Make sure you know what they are going to abbreviate and that you consider it appropriate.

Photographs

If you intend to include a photograph in your advertisement, or in a description of your home, then be careful how you tackle it. Don't take the picture 'straight on'. Stand slightly to one side. Make sure there are no cars parked outside or in the driveway and that the curtains are arranged neatly and evenly. Don't let anyone look out of the windows while you are taking the photograph. Avoid getting lamp-posts or trees in the centre of the picture. If the property is one of a terrace, don't take the whole row or no one will know which is yours. Try and choose a bright day (and don't forget those hanging baskets), mow the lawn, remove the rubbish or children's toys and make the whole property look at its best. It is wise to take photographs from several different angles before you decide which is the best. Mind the traffic if you have to stand in the roadway to get a good angle!

Providing written details

It is a criminal offence under the Trade Description Act of 1968 to make a false statement of fact in order to persuade someone to enter into a contract. You will find that all estate agents print somewhere on their specifications a statement to the effect that they do not form part of a contract, that the accuracy of the detail is not guaranteed although it is produced in good faith, and that the readers must satisfy themselves as to the accuracy of any statement made.

This is the sort of statement (or disclaimer) which makes it quite clear to the reader that the agent has no intention of misleading buyers or misrepresenting the property in such a way as to persuade the applicant to enter into any form of contract. A reputable estate agent will certainly not include any details on the specifications which are untrue or totally misleading – despite the jargon!

If you do not feel able to cope with this, or you are anxious about the legal implications of the Act, then do not bother to produce details of your home to give to prospective buyers, but you may consider that having written details ready might be beneficial. It will certainly give your viewers something to take away and remember you by.

You need not produce anything like an estate agent's specification: agents are experts and you are probably not. But let us look at some ideas which will help you to make up adequate details to hand to viewers.

- Head the specification *For Sale by Private Treaty*
- Next, give the full address of the property
- State the price and whether leasehold or freehold
- Describe the property briefly: for example, 4-bedroomed detached house, built 1965, offered in good decorative order and situated in quiet close
- Name each room in turn, starting on the ground floor and working upwards; give size and describe briefly what is in the room and any special features it may have, especially the kitchen if you intend to leave cookers, ovens etc.

- Describe the garden and include any sheds or outbuildings which are to remain; give size if known

- Make a separate note of the garage and any special features it may have

- Mention type of central heating installed

- Describe all other special features, such as cavity-wall insulation, recently rewired

- If the property is leasehold, state ground rent payable and any other related charges

- Give brief instructions on how to find the property

- Make a note of viewing arrangements which are convenient for you: for example, 'evenings or weekends by appointment by telephoning vendor on —'

- If carpets and curtains are *included* in the price, say so; but on no account include anything which you do *not* intend to include and leave behind. (You can negotiate the sale of fixtures and fittings later on if you need to)

- Include rateable value and rates payable (general and water)

- Add a disclaimer similar to the following:

  These particulars are supplied as a guide only, and their accuracy is not guaranteed, nor do they form any part of an agreement or contract. Viewers must satisfy themselves as to the accuracy of any statements made herein.

Keep the details brief and concise. Don't use jargon. Most importantly, *don't* lie or make any untrue claims. Never try and mislead people. You'll never make a sale if you do. It is better to mention that the house needs decorating than to say it is in excellent decorative order if it is not – better still, don't mention the décor at all if it really is that bad!

You will find that most photographers will prepare mini-prints of your photograph. These are supplied with tear-off sticky backs and can be attached to the details. Written details should be well presented and should not contain spelling or typing errors. You are trying to make an impression – you won't do so if you present poor-quality hand-outs.

Fixtures and fittings

We have already discussed this briefly, but at this stage it is very important that you decide exactly which fixtures and fittings you intend to include in your asking price and which you want to sell separately.

Make two lists for ease of reference – the first stating quite clearly what is to be left, and the second showing the items you have for sale, with an indication of the sort of price you hope to get for each one. You can then present these to prospective buyers when the time comes. If your eventual buyer wants to purchase specific items from you, you can list these and the price agreed, keep a copy for yourself and hand one to the buyer. The solicitors will probably want a copy, too. If you sort it out right at the beginning of your negotiations, there can be no query later on.

Conclusion

The world of advertising is a specialised one and unless it is an area which you deal with regularly, it can be a very difficult one to move into. It is, therefore, extremely important that you don't just throw together the first words you think of and consider them to be adequate. You must prepare carefully. Scan advertisements in all types of papers and magazines and establish some sort of example on which you can base your own.

You are unlikely to want to lavish a great deal of money on advertising, which is, after all, an expensive medium. Nevertheless, you *must* make an impact if you want to catch the eye of buyers. You need to think about the sort of person who is likely to buy your house (for example, first-time buyer, family, older people of retirement age, city workers, commuters) and gear the advertisement towards that type of buyer. Price and area are important too, though for security reasons, don't include your full address.

Finally, check the response to your first advertisement. As we mentioned earlier, if it is limited, reconsider the layout and wording of your advertisement; make adjustments and try again. If there is still no response, it is probably because the property is too expensive for the type of home it is, so look again at your asking price and the

the lowest price you have decided you will accept, and see if there is room to drop the marketing price. Whatever you do, *don't give up*. If the price is right, the house *will* sell.

5.
RECEIVING ENQUIRIES

Having placed your advertisements and perhaps sited a For Sale sign in your garden, you will soon start to receive enquiries from prospective purchasers. The way you deal with them could make or break your sale.

We mentioned earlier that positive responses to questions and knowing all the details about what you have to sell are important, and that it is necessary to be prepared for any questions that might come up. You should also be prepared to tackle enquiries from people who are only being nosy. Also, you should know how to deal with estate agents who might be touting for business.

Taking details from callers and making appointments

Let us start by discussing the most efficient way to deal with telephone calls in response to advertisements.

Hopefully, most of the enquiries will be from genuine buyers. Unfortunately, there are many people who will simply want to know where this nice house that is being advertised is situated, although they have no intention of buying. Some of them will probably be ringing just to get an idea of the value of their own home in comparison.

Have a notepad and pen by the telephone, together with a copy of the specification you have prepared. The very first question to ask your caller is his or her name and telephone number.' If they are reluctant to give you this, it will probably be because the call is not from a genuine buyer.

A word of warning: *never* give out your full address unless the caller is prepared to give you his or her name and telephone number. If he or she gives you this information, you can be pretty sure they are not a time-waster. If you are uncertain about the caller, try something along the following lines: 'I'm sorry I can't give you all the details right now. I have someone with me. But if you let me have your name and telephone number, I will ring you back in a few moments.' If the caller says you can ring back, then you're on the right track.

Be positive in your approach. If you feel the caller is really interested, describe the property in detail. You can give room sizes from your details and take the opportunity to point out any special features which make your house just that bit better than others. Don't overdo it though, or you will probably put the caller off! Give a good idea of the location of the property, but it's not wise to give out your full address until you are quite sure the caller is interested.

Try to get a positive commitment for a viewing before the caller rings off. Tell him or her that you have received several enquiries and if they are interested in viewing, they should come along immediately. Suggest a time and date and ask them to come along then. Don't let the caller go until an appointment has been made.

If the caller seems genuine but cannot make an immediate viewing appointment, arrange to send him or her a copy of the details you have prepared. Get it in the post the same day and if you don't hear anything after a couple of days, ring him or her up and ask if they are interested and would like to make an appointment to view.

It is important to keep a careful record of everyone who has contacted you, as well as those people who are coming to look round and what time they are arriving. Leave at least half an hour between appointments, if you can. There is nothing more embarrassing than two viewers arriving at the same time. If possible, make appointments during daylight hours. Bear in mind, though, that you might have someone wanting to visit right away, whatever time of day it happens to be. If they are that keen – *get them round immediately*. Don't put people off by being difficult over the time of their appointment. It is up to you to put yourself out as necessary. The viewer won't. He or she will simply not bother and look elsewhere.

As a precautionary measure, make arrangements for viewing when you are not in the house alone, especially if you are female.

It is important to take the name, address and telephone number of people who knock on your door in response to your For Sale sign. If they do call at an inconvenient moment, then you could ask them to make an appointment for later on, but as we pointed out earlier, if you put up a sign, be prepared to have callers at all sorts of odd times. It is best to show them around then and there too, regardless of whether or not you have made the beds and finished the washing-up, but apply the same criteria with regard to security – take names, telephone numbers and addresses and make sure you are not alone in the house. Don't let anyone in until you know who they are and where they are from.

Dealing with estate agents who call

The business of 'touting' by estate agents is generally frowned upon – not only by the public, but within the profession as a whole. However, that is not to say that it is a practice which does not go on. In fact, one could argue that, in order to stimulate business, an agent would be foolish not to overlook any opportunity to gain business.

Some agents will not approach you in person, but drop a letter through your door in response to your For Sale sign, asking if they can offer you their services, in which case it's up to you whether to reply or not. Others might be brash enough to hammer on the door or telephone in response to your advertisement, and tell you that they have an applicant on their books who is anxious to buy a house identical to yours. Now this could possibly be true! To find out, ask the agent what special reduced commission he would charge if this person were to buy. If it is low enough for you to accept, make it clear that this applicant is the only one you are prepared to allow to view – and that, only after the agent's fee and the 'one-off' arrangement has been confirmed in writing to you.

There is absolutely no reason why you should not try to sell your home yourself, while at the same time instructing an agent to sell it too. However, this can lead to a great deal of confusion and must be approached with caution. For instance, how can you claim a private sale if the agent has his board in your garden? He will argue that your purchaser was attracted to his sign and made the approach to you as a direct result of spotting the sign. Therefore, he has been instrumental in introducing the buyer to your home – for which his commission becomes payable. The solution is *not* to have an agent's board erected if you are trying to sell privately at the same time.

It is fair to assume, too, that genuine buyers will not only be looking for private advertisements for property, but they will also be 'doing the rounds' of local estate agents. They will probably be registered on agents' mailing lists and if you have given the agent instructions to sell for you, he may even have given the applicant a copy of your specification *before* the applicant replied to your private advertisement. In this case, the agent can, and most certainly will, claim that he (the agent) made the initial introduction – for which his commission becomes payable.

From your point of view, however, in both the above examples you could counter-argue that *you* negotiated the deal and showed the buyer round the property when, in fact, you had employed the agent to do so on your behalf. Therefore, surely, he has failed to some extent to carry out his duties fully? A reputable agent will probably offer to reduce his previously agreed commission rate in circumstances such as these. Nevertheless, it is a difficult and frustrating situation which, with a little thought, could easily be avoided. The best way is to make a careful note of the name, telephone number and address of everyone who approaches you direct and ask each applicant whether or not he or she has already been told about your property by the agent, or has registered with the agent. If he or she has, then it is safer to direct them back to the agent to make a viewing appointment, or show them around on the understanding that the agent will carry out the negotiations on your behalf.

As you can see, it is far better to sell your house privately and *not* instruct an agent at the same time. But be prepared for agents to contact you, and if they do, either tell them directly that you don't need them, or ask them what their lowest commission rate is going to be. If this seems acceptable and you agree that they can sell on your behalf, make it clear that you still intend to offer the property yourself, and follow the steps discussed above.

It should be noted that under the Estate Agents Act 1979, agents must tell their clients what they are going to charge and under what circumstances those charges become payable. This means that if you instruct an agent and he does not confirm what his charges are going to be, he could lose his legal right to claim them.

Taking security measures

Be careful about giving out your address too freely. Try to establish that the caller is genuinely interested before you tell him or her your full address. Do that and you should have no problems, but if the caller asks whether you live alone, or any other questions which do not seem to relate to their interest in the property itself, put down the phone.

Make sure there is someone else in the house as well as yourself when you show people around. That doesn't mean to say that you should both show them round, merely that there is someone else present.

If you live alone, get a friend to stay. If you are elderly, perhaps a friend or relative will show the prospective buyer around for you.

You can never be too careful. If you are really nervous, get an agent to act for you and make sure he or she always accompanies viewers.

Always make sure you know exactly who is coming and that you have a record of their address and telephone number for reference. Don't allow anyone in unless they are prepared to give you that information.

Conclusion

Sorting out the genuine buyers from people who ring out of curiosity is not easy, but if you apply the rule that if they are prepared to give you their name, address and telephone number, you can be fairly sure they are not totally wasting your time and you won't go far wrong. Be positive in your response to enquiries and suggest a time and day for callers to view without leaving it to them to do so.

As for agents, it is fair to say that most of them do follow up private advertisements with a view to persuading the seller to give them the instruction. If you decide to instruct an agent as well as try to sell your home yourself, make sure you follow the advice given and try at all costs to avoid a situation where an agent might be able to claim for his or her commission even though you conducted the sale yourself.

Finally, the matter of security. Fortunately, problems occur very rarely indeed, but bear in mind that prevention is better than cure!

6.
SHOWING
PEOPLE AROUND

Preparing your home

We have already discussed the presentation of your house with regard to maintenance, and pointed out that once you start to show people round it's far too late to say: 'Well, we intend to decorate this room – we just haven't got round to it yet.' The impression people get of your home is what they see then and there. If you intended to decorate, it should have been finished by now. Any work outstanding will only give your prospective buyer a point on which to base a much lower offer.

Keep rooms tidy – that's essential. The smell of polish helps, too, and there is nothing more attractive than fresh flowers dotted around the house. The bathroom should be spotless and put away toothbrushes and any other toiletries lined up on window sills or around the bath. In fact, put away everything throughout the house that may appear to clutter up shelves or window sills, or lie about rooms without adding to the presentation of the room itself. Small rooms, especially, need to be as free from clutter and unnecessary furniture as possible – this only serves to make the room look even smaller!

Clean windows. Make sure the kitchen is spotless – no dirty crockery lying around – and make quite sure that any fitted kitchen equipment, such as ovens and hobs, is as clean as possible. Tidy larders and any fitted cupboards, especially airing cupboards, and be prepared to have viewers peering into them. Fitted cupboards, after all, come with the house and are a benefit to the occupier, so they are bound to be inspected.

If you own pets, especially dogs, keep them in the garden when you have callers. Not everyone likes to be licked even if you do, and if the dog is in the least bit fierce or barks at visitors, keep it at bay!

Don't leave the children's toys lying around in every room. Keep them to one room if they must be lying around at all and make sure there is nothing on the floor which a viewer might trip over. Unfortunately, elderly bedridden relatives or a sick room do little to brighten the appearance of property, so add a few flowers and, if convenient, leave curtains open and put the lightest coloured bed-linen you have on the bed – do anything you can to make a sick room look light and airy.

Don't leave prams or bicycles inside the house. If you have a coat-stand, only keep the minimum number of items on it.

With regard to the outside, keep the garden tidy – especially where the dog might have been. If possible, avoid having washing on the line when viewers call.

The aim of the exercise is to present your property looking light and airy, clean and welcoming. Flowers help a lot and, as we have already mentioned, scented soap in bathrooms. Some people recommend the smell of baking bread too, just to make the house feel like 'home'. But, of course, not all of us are good at making bread! The secret is to make your home welcoming – a place where people *want* to live. If a home *feels* right, you are well on the way to making a sale.

Finally, pay special attention to your front door – outside first – and your hallway. These are often rather neglected areas of the home, yet they are obviously the first part of the house viewers are going to see. Be *especially* critical here. Throw away that old rug by the front door, polish the brass door furniture and the door itself. Wipe off the step and don't leave shoes or anything else lying around in the hallway. *First impressions count.* If viewers are put off by the entrance itself, they will not easily be impressed by anything else!

If you find people turning up outside, but not calling in, then you need to look again at the outside. Be critical. Are there any loose roof tiles which can be seen from the road? Does the fence need painting? Is there a dustbin in sight? Is the outside light not working? Are there too many cars about? Make sure yours is in the garage and try to avoid people parking directly outside – unless of course it is your viewer. Buyers look for clear access to property, especially if there is a shared driveway or communal access to garages.

It is difficult to keep your home extra tidy at all times, but when you are trying to sell, and you could have someone anxious to call right away, the effort must be made.

What questions are you likely to be asked?

It is obviously impossible to predict every one! However, if you did your homework as outlined in the previous chapters, you will have all the background information necessary to tackle most of the questions that are likely to be fired at you. For ease of reference, the following list of questions has been provided and includes all the topics we have discussed so far. You may like to make a note of the answers before anyone calls. Remember, you must always be positive when you are trying to make a sale. You won't make much of an impression if you are unable to give your viewers all the information they need, especially if that information is all that is necessary to clinch the deal right away. If you have to 'find out and let you know later', you're already too late!

Leasehold property, flats and maisonettes

- How much is the ground rent?
- How many years are left on the lease?
- Are there any maintenance charges? If so, what are they for and how much are they?
- Are there any other charges I should know about?
- What communal areas and facilities are there?
- Who maintains the shared facilities and is it done properly?
- Who is responsible for the upkeep of the outside of the building and the roof, and are things like painting the outside of windows done on a regular basis?
- The outside paintwork looks pretty grim – when is it due to be done again?
- Is there a garden and if so, which one is it?
- Is there a garage and if so, which one is it?
- Is the garage included in the price, or is it rented?
- If the garage is rented, how much is it going to cost?
- What other parking facilities are available, especially for visitors?
- I drive a lorry. Is there any reason why I should not leave it parked outside when I'm home?

- What happens if fire from an adjoining flat damages this one?
- Do you hear much noise from adjoining flats?
- Can I keep my dog and pet snake here?
- Where can I empty my rubbish and do I have to supply my own dustbin?

All types of property and general questions

- You have double glazing. What type is it and is it guaranteed?
- This is an older house. Has it been rewired and if so, was it done by a professional electrician?
- There is a flat roof. What sort of maintenance does it require?
- There is no garage. Is there planning consent for one?
- I need to keep my caravan here. Is there any reason why I can't?
- Where is the boundary?
- There is a shared driveway. What are the responsibilities of the owners and is there always enough room to park and gain access?
- Who is responsible for keeping boundary fences/walls maintained?
- Can I lop those high trees overhanging the back wall from next door?
- There is a septic tank. How often is it emptied and does it cause any problems? Is there any likelihood of the property being connected to the main drainage system and if so, when?
- What are the neighbours like?
- Have the timbers been treated and if so, is the work guaranteed?
- What are the average running costs of gas, electricity, and central heating?
- Is the garden sunny?
- Where are the nearest schools?
- Where is the nearest bus stop?
- How long does it take to get to the nearest shops?

- What other facilities are in the area?
- Where is the nearest doctor and dentist? What are they like?
- Is there likely to be further residential development nearby?
- Is there any other development going on nearby?
- Are you leaving your TV aerial?
- What arrangements are you making about the phone?
- What fixtures and fittings do you intend to leave behind?
- Who built your extension and when? Is it under guarantee?
- Is there any outstanding planning consent and if so, what for?
- Who is responsible for the road outside and who has to cut the grass verge?
- What sort of offer would you consider?
- When can you move out?

Finally, try to think of the questions you asked when you moved in. Add these to your list, too, together with any other questions you would ask if you were a prospective buyer – and be honest. Don't leave out questions simply because you don't have the answer. Find the answer and *be prepared*.

Showing people round

Always greet your viewers with a smile, introduce yourself and call them by name. If it's raining, or even in the slightest bit gloomy, leave all the lights on, and make sure the house is warm, with a glowing fire if possible.

Start by showing them the most impressive room on the ground floor. As you move around the house, let your viewers go into the rooms first and stay by the door. Too many people in a room makes it look small and overcrowded. Only one person should show people around. Point out the best features of each room and any special feature of the property as a whole, such as nice sunny position, close to the shops, economical to heat, excellent view, secluded plot and so on. Sell the *benefits* the property will provide for the buyers, as well as the property itself. But don't chatter aimlessly or you will frighten them off. Answer questions knowledgeably and remember they may well have seen several other properties already. You need to make them feel especially at home in yours. If they have young children, you might point out that children of a similar age live nearby, or that there is a baby-sitting circle. Relate your remarks to your observation of the viewers and what you learn of their circumstances from conversation as you show them round. If they have elderly relatives (and you have done your homework thoroughly), you can tell them about local clubs and outings for the elderly; in fact, all those special bits of information that make an 'area' a 'community' – the *benefits* the family will gain if it buys *your* house: things that other sellers might not bother about, but important things that make all the difference.

You also need to be able to 'counter objections'. Objections usually fall into the following categories:

- Price objection
- Location objection
- Size objection.

As you show people round, you can point out that the marketing price of your home offers excellent value for money. If you took the advice offered in Chapter 1, you will have researched the market thoroughly before you set your asking price. Therefore, you should be fully aware of the competition you face. You are then in a knowledgeable position to say that your property is good value, so countering a price objection before it arises.

Location objections can take many forms: too near a busy main road; a railway line running close to the back garden; too far for the viewer to travel to work. But if you think about it, each of these objections can also be countered. A main road, for instance, gives easy access for travelling to and from work, or for public transport. So, too, can a railway line. Living some way from a place of work can be something of a relief! It's nice to make a clean break at 5.30 pm!

If your home is small, it is probably cosy and easy to keep tidy and clean. Heating bills will be lower, too. Perhaps there is room to extend?

As you can see, most objections can be dealt with effectively. If there are obvious points to which prospective buyers might object, don't give them the opportunity! Counter the objection in conversation as you show them round. 'We're very close to the railway line here, which is great for travelling – it avoids all those hold-ups on the motorway!'

Why not make a list of possible objections which could be raised, and think of a suitable 'counter' dialogue before you start showing people around. But here again, don't mislead them. Just turn negative dialogue into a positive and advantageous selling-point.

Finally, always give your viewers time to chat together out of your earshot. The best place is in the garden (unless it's raining, of course), and finish by inviting them to look round again. You may like to offer them tea or coffee. This gives them an oppportunity to get the *feel* of your sitting-room. It also gives you time to chat and draw the deal to a satisfactory close (see Chapter 7).

If a viewer is really anxious to buy, he or she will tell you immediately. If the viewer has doubts, now is the time to sort them out and go for a commitment to buy. If a viewer leaves without making a positive commitment, you will be very lucky to ever see him or her again.

The following are good examples of 'closing' narratives designed to persuade buyers to make up their minds:

> 'You certainly seemed to like the house Mr X, if we can agree on a price now, I can instruct my solicitor to contact yours right away.'

or

> 'I can see you are interested then Ms Y? My asking price is £60,000. As you can see, the house is worth it. I also intend to leave the carpets and curtains [or other fixtures and fittings] in that price, so it is a very good buy compared with other properties on the market at the moment. I'm sure you agree.'

If your viewer says he or she is 'going away to think about it', suggest a time for another viewing, and point out that other people will be coming around in the meantime.

If your viewer says he or she doesn't want to buy, ask them why. You can learn a lot from other people's observations of your home. Maybe there's something you can do to improve things before the next viewer arrives.

Selling vacant property

Where it has been necessary to move out before your home is sold, it is a good idea to leave the carpets and curtains just to make the place look a little more like home. Room fresheners and scented soaps will help to avoid a 'musty' smell. Make sure the garden is kept tidy and not left to overgrow. During winter months, if possible, leave the central heating on low. If the system is timed, a short period in the morning and again in the evening will keep the house aired and free from damp, but make sure someone comes in once or twice a week to check that all is well. If this is not possible, turn off all the water to avoid problems with frozen pipes and radiators. For security reasons, try and make arrangements for someone to keep an eye on the property if you can.

Arrive early for your viewing appointment. Throw open all the windows and doors to let in fresh air. Pick up all the post (which always accumulates in empty houses) and have a good look round to make sure everything is in order. *Never give anyone the key and allow them to look round on their own.*

Selling to sitting tenants

Selling a property with a sitting tenant is not always easy and much will depend upon the terms of the agreement made with the tenant, for example, the length of the tenancy, and the terms under which the rent may be reviewed. If it is a tenancy for life, it will be advisable to offer the property to the tenant, although usually this means negotiating a price somewhat lower than the norm. However, it is probably the easiest way to sell such a property.

Many properties with sitting tenants are put to auction in order to obtain the highest possible price, for which the services of a professionally qualified person will be required. If the tenant does not wish to buy the property himself, then you may decide this is the most satisfactory alternative to get the best possible price. Arrangements for the auction should be made through a member of the Incorporated Society of Valuers and Auctioneers (see Useful addresses section). You will find the names and addresses of those suitably qualified in your local Yellow Pages. Many estate agents are members of the ISVA, or will be able to put you in touch with a member who will arrange the auction for you.

Auctions

An in-depth specification of your property will be drawn up, which will include details of any special terms and conditions which apply. You will need to contact your solicitor and advise him or her of the sale by auction so that the necessary information can be made available.

Prospective buyers must be allowed to inspect the property prior to the auction itself, so that they can arrange their finance. If a bid is accepted, the buyer must be in a position to sign the required documentation there and then. This document is, in effect, a contract and the buyer must pay a 10 per cent deposit, immediately making the matter legally binding.

You can set a minimum figure you require for the property, so that it can be withdrawn if that figure is not reached. You can also include on the details 'unless previously sold by private treaty', so that any interested party can make an offer prior to the date of the auction, giving you the opportunity to accept such an offer should it provide an acceptable figure.

The main advantage is, of course, that as soon as a bid is accepted at auction, the same position as 'exchange of contracts' is reached, where neither party may withdraw from the agreement. This can alleviate much of the anxiety of the 'chain' situation, while at the same time ensuring that the highest possible price is obtained for the property.

Analysing response

If you have a number of people looking at your home, but no one making an offer, even though the market generally is moving fairly quickly, it is probably because the price is wrong. If the price is within reason, people will make you offers. If they feel it is over-priced to such an extent that even a 'near-offer' won't make it realistic, then they won't bother, especially if there are other similar properties for sale that are cheaper anyway.

Then there is the question of presentation. Where there is a lot of response, but no offers, take another look around. What can you do to improve presentation? What is putting people off? You can improve your home, but you can't improve its location. If this seems to be the problem, sadly it must be reflected in the price, as we discussed in Chapter 1.

Where there is no response at all, it could be due to a general lack of buoyancy within the market as a whole, or again, that the price is wrong.

Try advertising again. Extend your advertising, too: if you used the classified section last time, use a full display now. Change the wording of the advertisement. Maybe you're not making the property sound interesting enough, or selling the special benefits your home has to offer. Only lower the marketing price when you have exhausted every other avenue open to you.

Conclusion

It is very difficult to keep your home neat and tidy all the time. Nevertheless, because it is important to show people round as soon as possible and not give them time to make viewing arrangements elsewhere, you must make the effort, and if they want to come round right away, let them.

Don't be too 'gushing' as you show people round. Remember to tell them what they will gain from buying *your* house as opposed to any other. Always smile, even on a bad day, and tie up the viewing by obtaining a positive reaction from the viewer. A definite No is better than 'We'll let you know later'. They never do!

7.
DEALING WITH OFFERS

It is all very well receiving offers for your home, but they must be acceptable and the buyer must be in a position to complete the purchase without any problems and without holding up any purchase you are making. It is a waste of time and effort to sell to someone unless you have checked that he or she is in the strongest possible position to complete the deal. Of course, it is not possible to predict every eventuality; but nevertheless there are steps you can take to find out, as far as possible, all you can about the buyer and his or her buying capability. The aim is to negotiate a sale which will complete as quickly as possible, and without too many problems or difficulties.

Who makes a good buyer?

Let us start by deciding who is most likely to complete the deal once it is under way.

As we have already discussed, a first-time buyer with a mortgage arranged in principle, and who is able to offer you written evidence of it from the lender, is always a good bet.

So, too, is a buyer who has already exchanged contracts on the sale of his or her existing home and who has also arranged a mortgage in principle.

A cash buyer who has already exchanged contracts on a sale, or who has nothing to sell anyway, is another good bet. However, a cash buyer whose money only comes through after he or she has sold another property, is unlikely to prove any more secure than someone who has still to arrange a mortgage.

Don't be frightened to ask a prospective buyer questions. You need to find out as much as you can *before* you agree the sale. You will find that many people are quite happy to discuss their position in polite conversation as they look around the house. Others, of course, are more difficult, and in some cases you cannot delve too deeply unless the viewer gets to a point where he or she makes you an offer.

If the purchaser is really keen, he or she will want to assure you that they are willing and *able* to buy and will probably give you all the information you need anyway, but you must satisfy yourself that the information is correct and that you are not being misled. Unfortunately, there are still buyers prepared to mislead sellers just to secure the property for themselves. Also, there are always those buyers who really have no idea what is involved, nor do they prepare themselves properly, so that when it comes to the crunch, they find they are not in a position to buy anything at all! As you can see, it rests with you as the seller to satisfy yourself that you are arranging a sale to someone who stands a good chance of completing the deal.

Here is a helpful guide to give you an idea of the information you need and the questions to ask your prospective buyer:

1. Is the interested party a first-time buyer? If so, has he or she already arranged a mortgage 'in principle'? Ask to see written confirmation of the arrangement. If there is none, suggest that the buyer makes immediate contact with a lender and lets you know, as soon as possible, whether a mortgage is likely to be obtained or not. In the meantime, keep your home on the market.

2. If the buyer says he or she is a 'cash' buyer, does that mean they can proceed right away, or are they still relying on the sale of another property? If the buyer still has a house to sell, keep yours on the market. Bear in mind that a cash buyer will still want to have your property surveyed.

3. If the buyer has already sold a property and exchanged contracts, you need to find out if they have already arranged a mortgage in principle (as above), or if they still have to make arrangements for their advance. A person will be a fairly reliable buyer if he or she has already arranged a mortgage, subject to survey, and can offer you some indication of a completion date which is in line with any dates you have in mind for your new purchase.

4. Be wary of agreeing a sale to anyone who still has a property

to sell. Such people will assure you that they will have no problems selling – the agent told them so! Don't believe it until it happens. Tell them to come back again when they have found a buyer. Better still, assure them that you understand their position, but you are not prepared to take your home off the market until they come up with a buyer for theirs. Don't frighten them off though – assure them that you will keep them fully informed of your position and hope they will be able to sell quickly, at which time you look forward to hearing from them again.

5. If your buyer says their house is already on the market, try to establish the sort of response they have received and the length of time the property has been for sale. If it has remained unsold for a lengthy period, assume there is a problem and don't finalise the sale. If they say they have several interested parties, or that they are 'about to exchange contracts', ask for full details of the chain: how many people are involved, how many have already obtained their finance, when exchange is likely to take place and as much information as you can. Again, don't finalise the arrangement and take your home off the market. Make it clear that you will keep the prospective buyer informed of your own position, but that you are not prepared to finalise a sale until they have exchanged contracts on their own sale.

6. Earlier in the book we discussed the mortgageability of property and the type of property on which lenders sometimes impose restrictions. Remember, when you are analysing the ability of your prospective buyer to complete the deal, that should they need to borrow a very high percentage of the total purchase price, and you feel your property falls into one of the categories on which lenders may restrict advances, the chances are there could be a problem, which might only come to light after a survey has been carried out. It is, of course, difficult to ask someone how much money they need to borrow from a building society. On the other hand, you can usually assume that a first-time buyer will want to borrow as much as possible and if you know this could pose a problem, keep your home on the market until the buyer has received an acceptable mortgage offer.

Don't finalise a deal with anyone unless you are convinced that he or she can complete the transaction. The problem is that such buyers are very few and far between, so the best course of action, when you find someone promising, is to offer them *first refusal*. This means that you will still offer your property, but that you will not agree a sale to anyone else unless they are in a much stronger position than the first buyer, and only if the first buyer is still not in a position to proceed to exchange of contracts.

If you are in any doubt at all, keep your home on the market and let the interested party contact you again when their position has improved.

Whatever information the buyer gives you, take it down in note form. Take the names and addresses of any estate agents involved, together with the name and address of the buyer's solicitor. Pass this information on to your own solicitor, who will then be able to check out facts and confirm – or otherwise – whether or not you stand a good chance of completing the deal.

The time factor

Much of your negotiation will be influenced by the time factor in which you have to work. For instance, you may lose the house you want to buy if you can't exchange and complete the deal by a certain date. This means that you will need to sell to someone who is also able to work within the time available.

If your buyer has exchanged contracts on their own sale, they will already have a date to work to. A first-time buyer, with a mortgage arranged in principle, should only be left with a survey to arrange and the legal side to be completed by his or her solicitor, which shouldn't take too long, but anyone else could well find it difficult to meet deadlines.

Where such tight time factors are involved, make quite sure you find out what, if any, time constraints apply to your buyer. If you are restricted over your own purchase, don't agree to an 'open-ended' sale and take your property off the market altogether, or you could find the whole thing going on and on with no sign of exchange, let alone completion in the foreseeable future.

Despite the complexity of tying up chains of sales which could consist of many properties and arranging completion dates which coincide and are convenient for everyone, solicitors usually manage it pretty well and you should be able to leave it up to your solicitor to sort dates out for you as soon as things get well under way. Nevertheless, it is a great help if you can come up with an anticipated date when you arrange the sale in the first place. That way everyone knows what they are aiming for and delays, if any, can be monitored and accounted for throughout the negotiations.

Negotiating a price

Having found someone anxious to buy and decided that, as far as you can find out, that person is in a good position to complete the transaction without too much trouble, the next step is to negotiate a mutually acceptable purchase price.

Nearly everyone nowadays makes an offer lower than the asking price, unless you have specifically asked for offers *above* a certain level, on receipt of which you will accept the highest, or unless there are several buyers all after the same property.

Let us look at some of the arguments on which buyers frequently base their offers and consider some of the responses you could use.

1. *A low offer is made because the property needs decorating.* You should have made allowances for this in the price, so you could argue that this fact has already been taken into account in the asking price and if Mr X compares your property with similar ones currently for sale, he can see that yours is already cheaper. Anyway, decorating it won't cost very much, so the property already offers excellent value for money.

   If Mr X persists, then you might consider a slight reduction for simple decoration based on, say, half the cost of the work; but don't do so unless the buyer can offer sound assurance that he can complete without any delay. If he can't, keep your home on the market and wait for more offers that could well be higher.

2. *Ms Y likes the house very much, but puts forward an objection based on size or location.* Here you must make it quite clear that she is unlikely to find such a nice property for the same price anywhere else. It really is excellent value for money.

3. *Mr A says he loves the house but he really can't afford it at*

the current price, although he can complete quickly. Now if he thinks this, he may not make you any offer at all because he believes he can't afford it, so it is up to you to suggest a price, especially if you have already established that he is a strong candidate to complete. 'I'm glad you like it Mr A. You certainly seem at home here and I'm sure you would be as happy here as we are. What if I were to reduce the asking price a little? I am sure we could come to some compromise.'

Suggest a very slight reduction at first and then negotiate further as necessary. As before, don't suggest a reduction when there is still a possibility of receiving higher offers from someone else.

4. *Mrs B makes a silly offer, but you have found out that she really is a good buyer.* 'I'm not prepared to accept that figure Mrs B, but as you are obviously so keen on the house, I could include carpets and curtains [or some other extra] which, as you know, are very expensive to replace nowadays.'

Again, only negotiate a reduced price if it is the only way to secure the sale.

5. You have not established whether Mr C is in a strong position to complete or not. Of course, in many cases the conversation cannot be brought around to discussing this point unless the viewer shows a keen interest in buying. Let us now assume that you know nothing about Mr C, but he wants to make you an offer.

'Well Mr C, I am certainly keen to negotiate a price with you and I am sure we can come to some mutually acceptable figure. However, I have received a great deal of response to my advertisement, and I am not prepared to consider an offer unless you can assure me that you are in a position to go ahead with the deal without any delays.'

Of course, the above are only suggestions, but hopefully they will give you an indication of how to deal with arguments. The secret is to negotiate a price which does not fall below your lowest pre-set figure and which takes into account the ability of the purchaser to complete the deal. If you take into consideration the type of objections that are likely to crop up and counter them in conversation as you show people around, you will find this very helpful too. It will go a long way to avoiding difficult confrontations when you come to close your sale.

Fixtures and fittings

Make sure your prospective buyer knows exactly what is to be included in the price and what you intend to sell privately.

If it means the difference between selling the property or not, consider *including* more extras to clinch the deal.

If your purchaser wants to buy any of the extras, provide a list and make a note of the agreed and accepted price for each item. Keep a copy of the list yourself and hand one to your purchaser. If you do this now, you will avoid any unnecessary misunderstandings later on.

Deposits

The purpose of a buyer leaving a deposit on a property is to indicate his or her intention to do their best to complete the deal. However, many transactions nowadays progress to completion without an initial deposit being pledged by the prospective buyer. An exception is new property, where developers still require holding deposits from prospective buyers. Where a deposit is lodged with an estate agent, that agent is legally obliged to hold the amount in a special clients' account. If the sale falls through, the money must be refunded in full.

As a private seller it is entirely up to you whether or not you take a deposit from your buyer. The simplest answer is not to, especially as the deposit itself is of little significance and forms no real part of a contract at this stage. However, a deposit certainly shows that the buyer is genuinely keen to complete and is probably less likely than some to let you down at the eleventh hour.

If you take a deposit yourself, make sure you provide a written receipt similar to the following:

> Received from Ms X [give her address] the sum
> of £xxxxx [in figures and in words] as a deposit
> in respect of her agreed purchase of [address of

property to be purchased] subject to contract and
survey.

Signed .... Dated ....

Pass the money on to your solicitor to hold as stakeholder. Your
solicitor will have a proper clients' account in which to keep it.
Better still, instruct your solicitor to ask for a deposit on your
behalf and let him or her deal with the whole thing for you.

If you really feel the need to ask your buyer to leave a holding
deposit to prove his or her interest to buy, discuss it with your
solicitor well before the event. Your solicitor will advise you as
to the way he or she expects you to go about it. Remember
that if the sale falls through, the deposit must be returned in
full.

A second string to your bow

Even the most straightforward deals can fall through because of
some completely unpredictable problem, so it is essential that you
don't take your property off the market until contracts have been
exchanged. Keep your options open and line up other buyers just
in case the first deal collapses.

Don't offer first refusal to anyone unless they really are the
best possible candidate to complete the deal. As we have
already discussed, where there is the slightest doubt, tell
the person to come back again when his or position has
improved.

Where you have a good buyer, offer first refusal, but continue to
show people around. Explain that there is an interested party who
wants to buy and is so far making good progress and that you will
contact the second, third or even fourth person if the deal should
fall through.

Keep a careful record of viewers and their telephone numbers,
so that you can contact them if your first sale starts to totter.
In Chapter 10, we will be looking further into the problems that
sometimes arise before contracts are exchanged, and discussing the
signs to look for that indicate a problem. These are the times when
you will need to contact other interested parties, so keep your lists
handy.

Gazumping

It is always tempting to accept a higher offer if one comes along, and there is certainly no reason why you should not do so. However, once a deal is under way, solicitors have been instructed and your prospective buyer has applied for his or her mortgage and arranged a survey, you are unlikely to find yourself at the top of the popularity poll if you then accept a higher offer. What you should do is to contact your first buyer and give him or her the opportunity of raising their offer to meet the new one. If the deal is in the very early stages and your second buyer can complete quickly, then you may decide to accept the second offer and cancel the first. However, if the first deal is making good progress, you will probably do better to stick with it. Alternatively, if both parties agree, turn the whole thing into a contract race...

Contract races

You can accept two or more offers, instruct solicitors accordingly and then complete the deal with the first of your buyers who is able to exchange the contracts.

Again, there is no reason why you should not do so, except that many buyers are unwilling to be part of a contract race and drop out even before it gets underway. Remember that where there is a race, someone will eventually lose and any expenses incurred will still have to be paid. From your point of view, however, it could be the solution where you have two or more people wanting to buy. You must tell everyone that they are in a race and make sure each of them is in full agreement. Bear in mind that once you mention *contract race*, all parties might withdraw from the deal and you could be left back at square one.

Bridging finance

It is sometimes possible for buyers to obtain bridging finance from their bank in order to complete their purchase before the sale of their existing home is complete. Some companies also offer bridging finance for employees moving to a new area.

Such extra finance is costly, both in terms of interest rates and the added expense of running two homes. If a prospective buyer says he or she can complete the transaction by raising a bridging loan, it is worth asking your solicitor to check with the buyer's solicitor that this is, in fact, correct. Proper applications must be made to the lender, and some may be unwilling to lend on an open-ended basis, so your buyer will need to have made enquiries well before he or she tells you they can certainly get the cash!

Bridging finance can also be raised in respect of the 10 per cent deposit required on exchange of contracts. Interest has to be paid on such a loan, and the lender will require confirmation that a contract is available. As a seller, your solicitor may be able to arrange for you to use the deposit your buyer pays you towards your own deposit on your new home. Ask your solicitor about this in advance.

Conclusion

It is important to handle your negotiations tactfully. Let us re-cap on the most important points to remember:

1. Find out as much about the viewer's buying potential in polite conversation as you show them around.

2. Counter potential objections *before* they are made.

3. Hold out for the asking price as long as you can and, in any event, don't drop below your lowest pre-set level.

4. Only agree a sale to a buyer who is in a strong position to complete.

5. Only resort to contract races if you have no alternative, or if you are not sure that your first buyer can complete.

6. Don't gazump a buyer without first giving him or her the opportunity to meet the higher offer, and then, only if the negotiations are not making progress.

7. Consider fixtures and fittings as a good point for negotiation.

8. Make sure you have other buyers lined up in case the first sale falls through.

9. Always let people know where they stand. If you have given someone first refusal, keep them fully informed of any other

interest. Make sure other interested parties know where they stand, too. You will lose sales if you play one buyer against another.

10. If in doubt, keep offering your home until contracts are exchanged.

8.
CONFIRMING
THE SALE

Now that you have found a buyer who is in a strong position to complete the deal and who has offered you an acceptable price for your home, the next step is to obtain written confirmation of all the relevant details in order to advise both your solicitor and the buyer's solicitor, and get the legal work under way without delay. Most of this information is best recorded in the form of a simple 'check list', along the lines of the following example which you can use yourself.

Full details of proposed property sale

Full address of property to be sold _____

_____

_____

Name(s) of seller _____

Address of seller if different from above _____

_____

_____

Telephone number of seller (home) _____

(business) _____

Name and address of seller's solicitor _____

_____

Name of contact solicitor within that company _____

Telephone number of solicitor _____

Full details of seller's intended purchase (include details of any chain beyond your purchase and any suggested completion dates if known)

_____

_____

_____

Name(s) of buyer _____

Address of buyer _____

_____

_____

Telephone number of buyer (home) _____

(business) _____

Contact name or telephone number buyer can use to arrange for a surveyor to call _____

Name and address of buyer's solicitor _____

_____

_____

Name of contact solicitor within that company _____

Telephone number of solicitor _____

Agreed and accepted price subject to contract and survey £ _____

Leasehold or freehold _____

If leasehold: number of years remaining on lease if known _____

Ground rent payable £ _____

Maintenance charges (if any) £ _____

Any other charges £ _____

Does the buyer require a mortgage? Yes/no _____

Has a mortgage already been agreed in principle? Yes/no _____

Name and address of buyer's lender _____

_____

_____

Full details of any 'chain' in which the buyer is involved (i.e., sold subject to contract, exchanged contracts, cash buyer). If selling agents are involved, include names, addresses and telephone numbers

_____

_____

_____

_____

Anticipated completion date _____

Deposit received £ _____ (send the cheque on to your solicitor to hold as stakeholder and provide the purchaser with a signed and dated receipt)

(Attach a copy of the list of any items the purchaser has agreed to buy, together with the agreed and accepted price for each)

Complete the above form and give a copy to the buyer whose own solicitor will also need the information. Keep a copy for yourself, too.

Sold subject to contract and survey

It has been argued that the term *sold subject to contract and survey* is of little significance today. However, it shows quite clearly that the deal has only been agreed subject to both parties signing an acceptable contract, and subject to the results of any survey the buyer may wish to have carried out.

It should be remembered that under English law, the transaction does not become legally binding to either party until the contracts have been signed and exchanged, and either party can withdraw from the deal at any point until then without penalty. There is certainly no harm in making this quite clear by using the term in any written document – including letters – you have to send prior to exchange of contracts.

Examples of letters confirming the deal

The following example letter can be used to confirm your acceptance of your buyer's offer, but don't forget to include *'subject to contract and survey'*.

Letter of confirmation to the buyer:-

Dear [name of buyer]

Re: [full address of property]

I wish to confirm that I am pleased to accept your offer of £xxxxx SUBJECT TO CONTRACT AND SURVEY for the above property.

Today I have contacted my solicitor [name and address of your solicitor] and instructed him to issue draft contracts to your solicitor [name and address of buyer's solicitor] as soon as possible.

I would ask you to keep me fully informed of your progress towards exchanging contracts, and trust that the transaction will reach a speedy and satisfactory completion.

If you have taken a deposit, add:

I also acknowledge receipt of your deposit in the sum of £xxxxx which I have today forwarded to my solicitor to hold as stakeholder in this transaction.

Letter of confirmation to your solicitor:

Dear Sirs

Re: [full address of property]

Please find enclosed, full details of the agreed sale for the above property to [name and address of buyer] SUBJECT TO CONTRACT AND SURVEY. Would you please issue a draft contract to [name of buyer's solicitor] as soon as possible.

(If you have taken a deposit, add here:

> I enclose a cheque in the sum of £xxxx which [name of buyer] has left as a deposit and would ask you to retain this as stakeholder in this transaction.)

> I confirm that this transaction was negotiated direct with [name of buyer] and no agent has been involved. I enclose, for information purposes, a list of fixtures and fittings [name of buyer] has agreed to purchase, together with the price offered and accepted.

Don't forget to keep copies of all your correspondence. Make sure the buyer and your solicitor both have copies of the list you made of extras, together with the price offered and accepted for each. A separate list of the items to be *included* in the price is helpful, too.

Conclusion

The law of contract is a complex one, so make sure you mark all correspondence prior to exchange of contract *'subject to contract and survey'*.

Gather as much information as you can at this early stage so that you are quite clear in your own mind the direction in which everyone is going. Ask the buyer if he or she can give you some idea when the surveyor for their lender is likely to call and don't be difficult over letting the surveyor gain access if you are working. Remember that if he can't get in when he needs to, it could be a while before he is in the area again and another appointment will have to be made. Such delays are unnecessary and only give rise to problems which could so easily be avoided.

Keep in contact with your buyer on a regular basis from now on, so that you always know exactly what is going on and what progress is being made. Don't leave it to the buyer to contact you – he or she will probably forget!

9.
WHAT THE SURVEYOR
WILL LOOK FOR

It would be very foolish for anyone to buy a property without having it surveyed. All buyers need to know that the home they are buying is in good structural order or, alternatively, if it is in poor condition, what the problems are and how severe each one is. All lenders will insist that a survey is carried out on the property requiring the mortgage anyway. There are different types of surveys and in this chapter we will look at each, so that you are fully aware as to what your buyer's surveyor will be looking for when he visits your home.

Basic valuation/inspection

When your buyer applies for his or her mortgage, their lender will require them to pay for a valuation to be carried out on the property – just as your own lender will if you are applying for a loan to purchase your new home.

The charge for this valuation is based on the price of the property. There is usually a choice as to the type of survey the applicant can opt for.

The lender will instruct a surveyor to carry out the valuation and he will usually contact you direct in order to arrange a mutually convenient time to call. Try and arrange it without delay. Don't cause any unnecessary hold-ups at your end, but bear in mind, that if you don't hear from either your buyer or a surveyor within a couple of weeks from arranging your sale, it is possible that your buyer is having trouble arranging his or her finance, and you will need to contact them to make sure all is well. If you still don't hear, yet your buyer insists that he or she has applied for their mortgage, then assume that there is a problem your buyer is not telling you about. You should ask your solicitor to make enquiries, too, especially if you are not able to find out anything positive yourself. In the meantime, keep your home on the open market.

The purpose of this valuation is for the surveyor to inspect your property to make sure it is worth at least the amount of money the buyer has applied for. The surveyor will put forward to the lender his valuation of your home. It will be this figure upon which the lender will base an offer of a loan to your buyer, and not necessarily the agreed selling price, unless it is lower than the valuation. The amount of money your buyer will be able to borrow will be a percentage of the valuation figure, usually up to 80 per cent. If your buyer needs to borrow a higher percentage of the valuation figure, he or she will need to take out additional security to cover the extra. This takes the form of a mortgage guarantee policy, for which the buyer will have to pay a single premium which is usually added to his loan. This policy covers the lender for any loss he might incur if the borrower should not repay the loan.

For the most basic inspection, the surveyor will be checking the property out for signs of damp, any obvious settlement or structural problems, and the condition of the property generally. He will take into account, when he considers the value, the location of the property and any known changes in the immediate vicinity which might affect the property in the future. If the home is leasehold, the terms and conditions of the lease will also be taken into account.

If the surveyor does not consider the property to be worth the amount of money applied for, he will *down-value* it, which means that your buyer may not be able to borrow as much as he or she wanted. In Chapter 10 we will be looking at this problem in more detail, and discussing ways in which you can renegotiate the sale in order not to lose your buyer.

A written report will be forwarded to the lender, a copy of which is usually sent to the buyer, too. As we have said, it will be the surveyor's appraisal of value or the asking price – whichever is the lower – upon which the final offer of a loan will be based.

We also mentioned earlier in the book that some lenders restrict their lending on certain types of property. If your home falls into one of the categories on which your buyer's particular lender is not prepared to offer a high percentage advance, that percentage will be based on the valuation figure. This is why it is so important to understand the types of restrictions which apply, and take this into account when you consider whether your particular buyer is in a good position to complete the deal.

House buyer's report and valuation

Your buyer might consider that a simple valuation will not be adequate, and you too may want a more in-depth survey to be carried out on the home you are buying.

The Royal Institution of Chartered Surveyors (see Useful addresses section) are able to offer the 'House Buyer's Report and Valuation', which can be arranged through any of their members. It is a survey which is adequate for modern houses and bungalows which are no more than 2,000 square feet in floor area and which are no more than three storeys high.

The surveyor will inspect all parts of the property to which he can gain easy access. He will not, for instance, move furniture or lift floor-boards, but he will check timber condition, damp, electrical fittings to which he can gain access, the condition of the roof, walls, sanitary-ware, plumbing, and the overall condition of the property. He will recommend further inspection by a professional specialist, such as an electrician or timber-treatment company, if he thinks this appropriate.

He will include in his final written report his estimate of value and will outline any problems which have come to light, and make recommendations as appropriate.

Flat buyer's report and valuation

This is also available through members of the Royal Institution of Chartered Surveyors and is similar to the above, but it is suitable for leasehold flats and maisonettes which are purpose-built or converted.

Here again, the surveyor will report on all parts of the property to which he is able to gain reasonable access. As he looks around, he may ask you about the general maintenance and upkeep of any communal parts of the property, and any obligations the occupant has towards them. If he has not received a copy of the lease, or is not familiar with it, he may also expect you to furnish him with certain details, such as the number of years remaining on the lease, or the terms of any insurance which covers the whole building and not just your part of it. This is where your 'homework', as we discussed in Chapters 1 and 2, is so very important.

The above surveys can be arranged privately or through the lender. If your buyer pays the appropriate fee, when he applies for his advance, the surveyor acting for the lender will carry out the report.

If, however, your buyer has decided to instruct a separate surveyor, then you can expect two surveyors to call. Make sure your buyer knows how you can be contacted to make the appropriate appointments.

Full structural survey

Your buyer might feel that he or she would prefer a full structural survey to be carried out. A professionally qualified surveyor is able to offer this service, but it is much more expensive than the other surveys we have mentioned. Fees are often based on the age of the property as well as the price.

Here, the surveyor will be looking into every nook and cranny of your home. He will be in the loft, peering under man-hole covers, poking around in the woodwork and all sorts of things. He will, in fact, identify every fault, however insignificant it may seem, and include it in his final report to your buyer.

The report will be a very comprehensive one, because if he overlooks any problems, which later come to light, he could well be sued for negligence, although it must be proved that he did not use the skills expected of a properly qualified surveyor if any law suit is likely to be successful.

A full structural survey may result in the buyer coming back to you complaining that there is far too much work to be done. The problem is that many of the faults identified are probably not too serious and likely to be found in most properties anyway. However, serious faults are often discovered, such as rising damp, the need for extensive timber treatment or underpinning – all of which are expensive to rectify. Ask to see a copy of the report so that you can assess exactly what the problems are and identify if there really is something seriously wrong.

Should you find yourself faced with a buyer threatening to withdraw from the deal because of the problems which have been discovered in the survey, or expecting to make you a very much lower offer, there are several courses of action open to you. Let us consider them in turn.

1. You can tell your buyer that you accounted for the general condition of the property in your original asking price. Therefore, the house, as it stands, is good value (as it should be, of course!).

2. If the above was not the case, then you might agree to a reduction in price to cover, say, half the cost, or at least a reasonable amount towards the cost of having the work done.

3. You may not wish to discuss the matter any further as you have already lined up another buyer who has not argued over the price anyway.

4. You can re-advertise and hope to find another buyer who will not require a full structural survey and, therefore, will not be frightened off by the discovery of defects which are likely to be found in most homes.

5. You may be just as surprised as the buyer to discover so much was wrong. In order to save the sale, obtain various quotations for getting the work done and come to a mutually agreeable arrangement with the buyer for paying for the work – again, perhaps by paying half or reducing the selling price by that amount.

These are, of course, only suggestions. Much will depend upon the circumstances at the time and the reaction of the prospective buyer. If the legal side of the transaction is well under way, and you have nearly reached a point where contracts can be exchanged, you will certainly not want to go right back to the beginning and start all over again. Therefore, if your buyer will only continue with the deal on the understanding that you reduce your price to cover the cost of the work, it is well worth renegotiating with him or her. But don't give in too quickly. If the problems are very serious, get your own estimates before you rush in and reduce the price. If they are not so serious, bear in mind that they will probably not cost too much to rectify anyway. Could you do it yourself without reducing the price?

Where your sale is still in its infancy, it could be wiser to re-offer in order to get the price you want. Some buyers are unwilling to go ahead with their purchase whether or not you suggest renegotiating the price. This is when you will benefit by having another purchaser waiting in the wings, ready to come on. This does not mean the problems with your property will go away, but it does give you the opportunity to tackle the work yourself, if this is appropriate. If the faults are likely to come up with every sale you make, it will certainly be beneficial to have the work done, or alternatively point out the defects to prospective purchasers and account for them in your asking price. Make this quite clear as people view. Point out that you are selling at a bargain price, and if they buy and have the work completed, the value of the property will soar. If they are made fully aware of the problem, they are far less likely to panic when they receive their surveyor's report and withdraw from the deal altogether.

If you do renegotiate a lower selling price, make sure you confirm it in writing to your buyer and to your solicitor immediately. Don't forget to keep copies of all your correspondence.

Conclusion

Earlier in this book we looked at the importance of presenting your home at its very best in order to obtain the highest possible price for it. As you can see, it is no good trying to cover up obvious defects that you know exist and which a surveyor will certainly notice. Far better to get the work done properly and reap the full reward in your eventual selling price.

If it is not practical for you to have the work completed, there is no harm in pointing out the more serious problems as people look around, and making it quite clear that the cost of the work has already been accounted for in the asking price. The property will, of course, be worth even more when the work is carried out, so you could turn the whole thing into a good selling-point, rather than a bad one. But remember that buyers are not fools, neither are surveyors, so don't try to pull the wool over their eyes. Be honest and be realistic in your negotiations and bear in mind that paint and paper will not cover up serious rising damp, dry or wet rot, or worse!

Here is a list of some of the more serious problems found in property today:

- *Wet rot*. Here the timber is completely saturated, breaking up the fibres of the wood and weakening it generally.

- *Dry rot*. A type of fungus which lives in very damp conditions and breaks up the timber by drying out the fibres. Damaged wood crumbles, almost powder-like, to the touch.

- *Woodworm*. This is the caterpillar of the beetle. It eats its way through timber. The tiny holes in woodwork are caused by the animal tunnelling its way out. Eggs are deposited within the holes.

Any of the above can cause general weakness of the timber and it is a good idea to seek professional advice about treatment and, if necessary, replacement.

- *Settlement*. Nearly all homes settle to a certain extent, usually shown by tiny cracks in the plasterwork, which once filled are unlikely to open further again. Check brickwork, however. Obvious cracks in outside walls, or your home leaning to one side, are potentially far more serious.

- *Rising damp*. This is usually due to a defect in the damp-proof course. You may need to call in a builder to knock out bricks and reinstate the damp-proof course itself – a costly business.

- *Roofing*. Make sure the roof is in a good state of repair. If there are signs of water penetration, ask a local roofing contractor to check it out.

10.
PROBLEM
SOLVING

Once you have agreed a sale and it is under way, it is important that you monitor its progress very carefully indeed. You need to keep in constant contact with your buyer and your solicitor to find out exactly what is happening and why. It's no good sitting back and expecting everything to fall smoothly into place because, unfortunately, the process of buying and selling property is rarely that simple.

If you are aware of what is going on and the reasons behind any action which is being taken, you can keep in control of the situation and take the necessary steps to make sure the sale goes through. You also need to identify any weak points in the sale and know how to tackle them in order to save the day. In this chapter, we will be looking at the most common problems which arise and discussing the options open to you in order to overcome them. Unfortunately, it is not easy to predict every possible problem, but those mentioned here cover the areas where many sales begin to totter, and include constructive ideas on what action to take to save your sale.

You need to remember that neither you nor your buyer is legally committed to completing the deal until the contracts have been signed and exchanged, so that even a simple change of mind from either one of you can make a difference. Problems occur, too, when buyers and sellers do not keep in touch and lose track of what the other is doing. Misunderstandings and bad feelings creep in. Then sheer frustration and disillusionment take over, often resulting in the sale falling through when, with a little more thought and effort from both parties, problems could have been solved and the deal forged ahead quickly and efficiently.

Knowing your own position

It is important to know your own position with regard to the house you are buying, especially if it involves a chain of sales beyond your purchase. You can then base the terms of your negotiations on that information. For instance, you may need to complete by a set date, so you may decide to accept an offer lower than the asking price from someone who can fall in line with that date. On the other hand, perhaps you have no exact date to work to because there is a delay in the chain beyond your purchase, in which case you may have time to hold out for your asking price.

If you are moving into a newly built property, you will probably have been given a fixed date by which to exchange contracts and complete the deal. Although developers are quick to set such tight deadlines, you need to keep a very careful eye on the progress of the building work, checking regularly that it is proceeding as planned and is not being held up for any reason. You will be offering an 'end of chain' position to anyone buying from you, but make sure that any suggested completion date you pass on to your own buyer is being upheld by the developer. If your own date is put back, you must let your purchaser know so that anticipated completion dates can be adjusted accordingly.

Things get slightly more complicated if you are buying from someone who is also buying from someone and so on. You will need to make sure everyone beyond your own purchase is about to, or has already, exchanged contracts and that some sort of realistic completion date has been established. Don't forget that anyone dropping out of, or causing a hold up to, that chain, can do a lot of damage to *your* sale, especially where everyone is relying on the next in line in order to make progress.

Of course, your solicitor will be keeping a careful eye on all this, too; but a friendly telephone call to the person selling to you, just to keep in touch and check that all is progressing well, will set your mind at rest. If you are buying from an agent, he or she should check on progress at regular intervals, too, so if you're not kept informed, find out why and insist that you are in future!

Many people are reluctant to put their home up for sale until they have found another one to move into, especially if they are not forced into the move by circumstance, such as a change of job location or something similar. The problem here is that if your new purchase is dependent upon the sale of your present home, you *must* sell in order to buy. As we discussed earlier, happily, most solicitors are able to sort out completion dates fairly satisfactorily, but it stands to reason that if your next purchase depends on selling your present home, you must get that home on the market as soon as you decide to move, whether it is a move from choice or otherwise, and whether or not you have found something to move into.

You will be in a much stronger position to bargain for any home you want to buy if you have already lined up a buyer for your existing property, just as you will appreciate receiving offers from prospective buyers for your home if they have already exchanged contracts on any sale they are making.

Once you have decided to move, get your home up for sale. If you haven't been lucky enough to find the right home to buy yet, just explain that to your prospective buyer. If he or she is keen to buy, they will be prepared to wait; if not, then they can look elsewhere – but at least get the ball rolling.

Tackling chains

Now let us look at problems which can arise from chains beyond your purchaser.

If you have followed the guide-lines laid down earlier in this book, you will hopefully have found a buyer who has already exchanged contracts on his or her sale, so there should be no difficulties there. But what sort of problems arise when your buyer still has a house to sell?

If you receive an offer from someone who has not yet sold their own property, don't just sit back and wait for them. Keep your home on the market and tell the person to come back when his or her position has improved. Even if the person *has* found a buyer, it is always possible that someone behind *his* sale has a problem. This often happens where long chains of sales and purchases are involved. Your prospective purchaser still wants to buy. His buyer still wants to buy from him, but beyond that . . .? If everyone has reached a point where they have found buyers and all have arranged mortgages, it is a very sad situation when just one person drops out – for whatever reason. Here again, you must line up someone else to buy from you. Whatever your feeling towards your buyer – he or she may even be pleading with you at the front door – if they can't offer you some end to the chain, perhaps by arranging bridging finance to complete their deal with you, you must keep your options open and not take your home off the market.

Where chains are involved, whether they consist of 2 or 20 people, only consider it safe to proceed with the deal if your prospective buyer is ready to exchange contracts on his sale, or can arrange bridging finance to do so. Keep your own property on the market until that time.

Down-valuations

As the market value of property continues to rise, the number of down-valuations seems to be growing, too. Estate agents and surveyors have made some attempt at stabilising prices, but the property market as a whole is such, that keeping prices level, or at least more attainable for ordinary home-buyers, is difficult – even for the professionals. Some might even argue that estate agents, when they value a property, are often tempted to over-price in order to get the instruction from the seller. Unfortunately, this is true in some cases. The problem is that when a surveyor calls at your property on behalf of your buyer's lender, he has to make sure that if the buyer does not keep up his or her mortgage repayments, the lender can resell the property and recoup the money outstanding. The value the surveyor places on the property takes this into account, assuming that it could happen immediately. He has to make sure the mortgage does not exceed the value of the property, so that if it were sold, the amount of the outstanding loan would not be realised.

This is all very well for him, but from your point of view, the selling-price you have negotiated should be a realistic one and one you want to get at the end of the day! So what happens if your buyer comes back to you threatening to withdraw from the deal because the valuation figure is lower than the agreed selling-price?

He or she will argue, of course, that the house isn't worth the agreed figure. The first thing to consider is how far the legal work has progressed at that point. If all is going well, there are no other hold-ups and all that is outstanding is the buyer getting his or her mortgage offer, you could renegotiate a slightly lower price, bearing in mind that to re-offer your home at this late stage is likely to be time-consuming and costly.

Your second option could be to split the difference between the valuation figure and the asking price, as long as this still affords you a realistic figure; or you could offer to leave extras, like curtains, carpets, etc., to make up the value. As a last resort, you might be willing to drop your price down to the valuation figure. However, don't do that unless there really is no alternative – much better, if you have time on your side, to put your home back on the market and try again, bearing in mind that if your next buyer applies for his or her mortgage from another lender, that surveyor may well come up with a higher valuation.

Retentions

A lender may be willing to advance the amount of money your buyer has applied for, but not until certain works are carried out to the property in order to bring it up to the correct value.

If this happens, the lender will withhold a certain amount of the advance, usually the amount the work will cost to carry out. This means that if the borrower is still willing to go ahead, the deal can be completed, but he or she will only receive part of their advance. The lender will list the work which has to be carried out and when the new owner takes occupation, he or she must arrange for it to be done. The surveyor then makes another inspection of the property, and if it is now up to the standard he is looking for, the remainder of the money will be advanced. Usually, borrowers who find themselves in this position are able to arrange a bridging loan to complete the purchase and do the work. This is paid off when the money retained is finally released by the lender.

However, this is another situation where buyers sometimes decide not to carry on with the purchase in the light of the work they will be expected to carry out. If this happens, your buyer may want to negotiate a drop in the agreed price by an amount to cover the cost of the repairs.

Here again, if all has proceeded well up to this point, you may decide to compromise over the price, perhaps by reducing the amount by a small proportion of the cost of the work. Alternatively, you could get your own estimate for the work. There is certainly no harm in doing this, especially if you consider the amount retained to be far more than the work would actually cost to do. If your estimate is lower, base your renegotiated price on that figure – or, of course, do the work yourself.

Your other alternative is just as before – put your home back on the market and hope your next buyer uses a different lender!

Effective follow-up

You need to keep a close eye on the progress of your sale at all times, so that you know exactly what is going on and where your sale currently stands. First and foremost, keep in contact with your buyer. Don't rely on him or her to contact you – they probably won't.

If you don't see a surveyor after the first couple of weeks, find out why. If your buyer hasn't bothered to apply for his or her mortgage by then, sell to someone else who is prepared to get a move-on. If your buyer says he has applied for a mortgage, make sure he confirms a definite date and time for the surveyor to call. If this still doesn't happen, assume the worst and contact other parties right away.

If your buyer is involved in a chain, your solicitor should be able to find out what position everyone is in with regard to getting their mortgages and how far the legal work has progressed. Ask him or her to let you know, too. If there is any link in the chain where a property has not yet been sold, or there is a problem with a mortgage, line up another buyer in a stronger position.

There is nothing more frustrating than long periods of silence when you don't hear from anyone. You always assume the worst even though the assumption may be unfounded, so if in doubt, contact your buyer and chase up your solicitor and insist that they keep you up to date.

If your solicitor is about to go on holiday, get him or her to instruct their secretary, or the person taking over their work, to keep you in the picture, too. Don't let your solicitor leave your file in his 'IN' tray, waiting unattended until he gets back!

If there is any potential problem, constant and friendly follow-up tactics with your buyer and your solicitor will bring it to light. Then you can make the necessary moves, such as issuing another contract to a second interested party, or withdrawing from the first deal and negotiating a sale to someone else. This shows the importance of keeping your options open at all times and lining up other buyers. Never rely on just one buyer. On the other hand, don't rush in to cancel one deal, especially if it is well under way, unless you are absolutely certain there is no alternative.

Remember, too, that if you decide to issue more than one contract, or cancel the deal and sell to someone else, you *must* liaise with everyone concerned and keep them all in the picture. If you don't, you'll probably end up with no sale at all.

Co-ordinating your purchase with your sale

If you are buying through an estate agent, he will want to know how your sale is progressing and make sure you can keep in line with any dates set by his client – the person selling to you. He will be monitoring things, just as you must too, so that if there is a potential hold-up at your end, he might well advise his client to sell to someone else.

Even where there is no selling agent and you are buying direct from the seller, the same criteria applies to you as it does to your buyer. If there is a potential hold-up, the vendor will undoubtedly find another buyer and you will be disappointed.

As you can see, your position is greatly strengthened if you can line up a good buyer before you commit yourself to another purchase. On the other hand, you may be lucky enough to be in a position to arrange a bridging loan. But this can be expensive – not a position to get in without careful budgeting and accounting.

If there is a hold-up in the chain beyond your buyer, but the legal work is well under way, you and your solicitor may be able to persuade the person selling to you to wait a little longer, until the problem is resolved. Much will depend upon the problem itself. For instance, if someone further down the chain has lost a buyer and has had to start from the beginning again, there is likely to be a long delay unless he or she can find a new buyer immediately.

It is certainly not a good idea to complete your purchase without completing your sale. In fact, solicitors are very careful to make sure both transactions complete on the same day. If by any chance you can only save your sale by moving out prior to buying another home, don't do so unless you have a definite completion date for your purchase, or alternative accommodation to move into, and then only after seeking advice from your solicitor.

Conclusion

The only way to make sure your deal continues to progress is to keep in regular contact with your buyer and your solicitor.

Don't be fobbed off with excuses. Take the initiative. If there is a problem which could well mean the deal will be extensively delayed or fall through altogether, contact the next interested person from the list you made as you showed people around, and get other contracts under way.

Don't let a prospective buyer withdraw from the sale without giving you a good reason. Of course, people do just change their minds, or see something else they prefer. Often they don't contact the sellers: they just leave a message through solicitors to say the deal is off. If this happens, there is probably little you can do, except perhaps to offer to sell at a reduced figure. But don't do that unless you have absolutely no alternative.

Don't accept someone withdrawing from the sale because of a retention or down-valuation without first finding out why this happened. Ask to see the surveyor's report and judge from that whether it is in your best interest to renegotiate a lower price or to hold out for the asking price and sell to someone else.

11.
THE LEGAL
FORMALITIES

It is important for all buyers and sellers to understand how the legal formalities of buying and selling a property are carried out and what is involved.

Having sold your property yourself, you may consider undertaking the legal work yourself, too, and there is certainly nothing to stop you. However, unless you have some previous knowledge of conveyancing, or can call on a reliable friend or colleague for help and advice, it is not a good idea to attempt such an important task on your own. The implications of making a mistake, even the smallest one, could be very serious indeed, even though you can save solicitor's and estate agent's fees.

The business of selling your home and finding a buyer is not a difficult one and, unlike conveyancing, it does not call for professional qualifications and several years of training backed by stringent examinations which must be passed. You might be able to handle the sale, but are you really competent enough to handle the contract yourself in view of the fact that you are unlikely to have the experience or have passed the required examinations?

If a solicitor fails to carry out his or her professional duties competently, you can claim for any loss you incur due to their professional negligence. This can be direct from the solicitor or through the Law Society's Indemnity Fund (see Useful addresses section), but if *you* make a mistake there is very little you can do about it! So don't take a chance – stick to the professionals and make sure you get the job done properly.

Conveyancers and solicitors

You will find the names and addresses of solicitors and conveyancing companies in your local Yellow Pages, or from your nearest Citizens' Advice Bureau.

You will probably have used a particular company when you purchased your home in the first place, so if you were satisfied with the service, and the company is local, you might want to use them again.

Conveyancing companies specialise only in conveyancing. In 1985, under the Administration of Justice Act, the Council for Licensed Conveyancers (see Useful addresses section) was established to supervise non-solicitor conveyancing. It expects conveyancers to undertake a proper training programme and to sit a series of examinations. So they, too, must be properly qualified licensed conveyancers before they can draw up conveyancing documents and, since December 1987, before they can draw up draft contracts. It is illegal for an unqualified person to carry out this work and charge a fee for doing so.

Shop around to find out the sort of charges you are going to have to pay for the work to be done. Compare solicitors' charges with conveyancers'. Find out if the charges are a *set* fee or just an estimate. Remember that there are a certain number of statutory charges which you will have to pay anyway, which we will be discussing in greater detail in Chapter 13.

It is a good idea to line up a solicitor or conveyancer before you begin the process of selling. If you are buying, too, you will probably have already done so anyway. Just let them know what you are doing and keep them in the picture. Send them all the relevant information (as in the check-list in Chapter 8) as soon as it is to hand. Keep in close contact with them as the legal work progresses to make sure all is going well, so that if there is a hold-up or problem, you can take the appropriate action as quickly as possible.

Making the enquiries

On receipt of your letter confirming your sale, your solicitor will draw up a draft contract and send it on to the buyer's solicitor. This is a document which could well be passed between the two solicitors on several occasions before its contents are finally approved and accepted.

It is the job of the buyer's solicitor to make sure you are legally entitled to sell the property in the first place and that there is nothing about the property, or which could affect the property in the future, which could make the new buyer's occupation unhappy and/or uncomfortable.

The buyer's solicitor will carry out 'preliminary enquiries' via your solicitor and yourself. A standard form can be used for this purpose, which will also include any additional questions the solicitor thinks appropriate. These questions relate to the property itself and include the following areas:

- Rights of way. What access is there to a rear entrance, for instance?

- Rights of way across the property and its land, called 'easements'. For example, a drainage system running across your land and the responsibility associated with it.

- Has planning consent been applied for and if so, what for?

- Have there been any alterations or extensions carried out to the building?

- Are there any shared rights of access: for example, a shared driveway? What are the responsibilities associated with it?

- Where is the boundary? Who is responsible for the upkeep of boundary fences or walls?

- Are there any 'restrictive covenants' which apply? These are things you *can't* do, like running a business from the property.

- Are there any 'positive covenants' which apply? These are actions or responsibilities the occupier *must* carry out.

- Are there any guarantees which apply to things like timber treatment or re-roofing?

- Is there any reason why the sale is being made which could result in there being a future problem over possession?

- Is any part of the property let?

The buyer's solicitor also makes 'local searches' through the local authority. Again, a standard list of questions is often used. These cover any changes to the local environment which might affect the occupation or value of the property in the future. This could be along the lines of a proposed motorway cutting across the back lawn or any other development planned for the neighbourhood.

Your solicitor will be able to answer most of the questions in respect of the preliminary enquiries he or she receives, but will probably pass on to you anything outstanding. One of the questions you will have to answer will be about what extras are to be included in the price, which are to be sold separately and for what price. This is where your previously prepared lists will come in handy.

If the buyer is not happy with some part of the information gathered, or raises an objection to a particular point, he or she may come back to you and expect to renegotiate the deal in the light of their findings. It is important that you consider very carefully what aspect is being queried. It could well be something which the two solicitors could sort out without the need for you to lower your price, so don't do so until you have discussed the matter in full with your own solicitor and discovered exactly what the problem is. It could be a legal point which the buyer doesn't fully understand, rather than a problem which can be resolved or accepted by the buyer only if you drop your price. If, however, it is something more serious, such as an impending compulsory-purchase order due to be slapped on the property by the local authority which you knew nothing about, then obviously the value of the property will be adversely affected and you will need to reassess your asking price. Fortunately, such problems rarely occur in practice, but if you are in any doubt, don't lower the price unless there is absolutely no alternative and then, only on the advice of your solicitor – assuming that it is a problem which he or she is unable to resolve.

Draft contract

As soon as all the enquiries are completed, two copies of the contract will be drawn up. The information contained in this document will include the following:

- The name of the buyer and the seller and their occupations
- The price agreed
- The address of the property and a description of it, including whether the property is leasehold or freehold (if it is leasehold, the date of the lease and other details relating to the lease will also be entered)
- Whether the seller sells as the owner, or in any other capacity
- The completion date
- The deposit, which is usually 10 per cent, but will take into account any smaller deposit your buyer has already left

- The title number of the property will be shown under the heading 'HM Land Registry' if the property is registered
- Whether the property is used as a family dwelling house or for any other purpose
- Whether the property is sold with vacant possession
- Details of covenants, conditions, declarations or any special agreements which might apply to the property
- Rate of interest which could be charged on unpaid purchase money, or if the completion is delayed for some reason
- A list of items to be purchased separately and the price

The legal jargon in which the document is written may not be clear to you. If you are in any doubt, ask your solicitor for a translation. In any event, *don't* sign anything unless you understand it fully.

Land registry

Every time a property is bought or sold and there is a change of ownership, solicitors have to check all the previous transactions on that property with the Land Registry Office.

All the details of previous owners, mortgages, rights of way and other details which apply to properties registered with the Land Registry Office are recorded and the accuracy of the records is guaranteed by the State.

Your buyer's solicitor will check the Land Registry to find out these details if your property is registered. If the property is unregistered, he or she will have to check the title deeds going back at least 15 years to establish what is termed a 'good root', and make sure you are entitled to sell the property.

Most homes in England and Wales are now registered, and each time there is a change of ownership, it must be recorded. If a property is unregistered when it is sold, a new entry must be made on the register.

The buyer must pay the registration fee, which is based on the price of the property. The amount is higher for a first registration than it is for a change to be made to a registered property.

From a seller's point of view, there is unlikely to be any problem at this point unless something completely unexpected comes up during the checking of the register or the title deeds.

Stamp duty

Currently (1988/89) stamp duty, which is a tax on certain legal documents, is 1 per cent of the total purchase price of a property over £30,000. It is the buyer who pays this amount and, as you can see, it can add a hefty amount of money on to a purchase above that figure.

Bearing in mind this extra cost to your buyer, if your property is on the market for around the £30,000 mark, and the additional cost of extras pushes it above that figure, you might suggest to the buyer that he pays for the extras as a separate amount so as not to increase the overall purchase price to the amount on which stamp duty becomes payable. It is a matter which the buyer's solicitor will consider, too, but it is a point worth bearing in mind when you sell your home, as it could mean the difference between a prospective buyer being able to afford the property or not.

Conveyancing and transfer documents

The legal work connected with buying and selling property is generally referred to as 'the conveyance' or 'conveyancing'. A *conveyance* is, in fact, the legal document which transfers ownership of a property to the buyer from the seller if the title of the property in question has not been registered. A *transfer* is the document which transfers the ownership when the property *has* been registered.

You will be required to sign these documents as the seller.

Exchanging the contracts

Up until this point, either party can withdraw from the deal, even if the buyer has left a holding deposit with you or your solicitor. However, once the contracts have been exchanged – which means exactly that: the two copies of the contracts are signed, one by the buyer and one by the seller, and the two solicitors exchange the copies and pass one on to the other – the matter then becomes legally binding to both parties.

The buyer must pay a deposit of 10 per cent of the purchase price on exchange of contracts. If he or she can't raise the full amount, they will probably be able to obtain a bridging loan, as we discussed earlier. The figure of 10 per cent can be reduced by arrangement and you can use the deposit received from your buyer towards your own deposit. Your solicitor will make the appropriate arrangements if such an agreement has been reached in your particular case.

Once contracts are exchanged and the deposit received, should the buyer then fail to complete the purchase, he or she will lose their deposit and you as the seller can claim for any outstanding money, together with any other financial loss you have incurred due to the buyer withdrawing.

As soon as exchange takes place, the buyer becomes responsible for insuring the property. His lender arranges the cover, which means that, if by chance the property is razed to the ground by fire or some other catastrophe between the point where contracts are exchanged and completion, it is the buyer who is covered by the appropriate insurance.

Exchange will not take place until all the preliminary enquiries and local searches have been completed satisfactorily, all queries have been dealt with, the buyer's mortgage has been granted in writing, the deposit has been paid and a date for completion has been agreed. Where the buyer is purchasing a newly built property, a National House Building Council agreement must also have been received.

If you are buying another home at the same time, your solicitor will endeavour to tie up the exchange of your contract to purchase with the exchange of your contract to sell. Where the funds raised from your sale are needed to complete your purchase, especially if you are unable to obtain a suitable bridging loan to complete the deal, your solicitor is unlikely to advise you to exchange contracts on your purchase until you have exchanged contracts on your sale. Likewise, he or she won't want to make you homeless either, and won't advise you to sign away your old home until you have somewhere else to go!

At this point, you can sit back and relax a little. Your sale has finally reached a point beyond which it is most unlikely to fall through!

Completion

A date for completion will have been agreed and included in the documentation. It is usually between four and six weeks after exchange. This is because there are a few formalities which the solicitors still have to complete, such as the buyer's solicitors preparing the transfer document and arranging for the money to be available on the right day.

Your solicitor will prepare a completion statement for the buyer showing the amount of money he has to pay together with any apportionment of outgoings, such as rates. It also includes the amount the buyer has to pay to your building society or other lender to discharge (pay off) your existing mortgage, and to whom this must be paid.

When the final payment has been received, your solicitor will hand over the deeds, which will include the conveyance or transfer which you have signed, in exchange for the money. The buyer's solicitor then arranges for the stamp duty to be paid and forwards the deeds to the buyer's mortgage lender, where they are kept as security for the money they have lent.

You must now move out and the new owner can move in.

Conclusion

Fortunately, you can leave all the worry of the legalities to your solicitor or conveyancer and let them sort it all out. Having said that, however, you still need to be kept in the picture.

As a private seller, you will be monitoring the progress of the sale carefully in order to spot any potential problems and take any action necessary to save the sale or, if the worst comes to the worst, to make a new sale. In order to do this efficiently, you will need to know how far the conveyance has progressed and if there are any difficulties, not only with your part of the contract, but also in relation to anyone else involved in your chain. Don't forget that it might not be you or even your buyer who causes the problem. It could be someone further down the line experiencing difficulties sorting out the conveyance or getting a mortgage. If it is, then your solicitor should know about it. In fact, he will probably find out before your buyer, so the information should come direct from him, together with advice on what action he or you should now be taking.

In the business of buying and selling property, time is usually a critical factor. It cannot be wasted by anyone. So if your solicitor doesn't keep you in the picture, contact him at regular intervals to find out what is going on. If he goes away on holiday, make sure there is someone dealing with your work who can keep you up to date. After all, that's an important part of the service you are paying for, especially as you are selling your home yourself.

Finally, here is a run-down of what your solicitor will be doing on your behalf:

- Receives your letter confirming full details of the agreed sale and accepts any deposit received as stakeholder
- Draws up the draft contract and sends it to the buyer's solicitor
- On receipt of enquiries from the buyer's solicitor, he will provide all the information required about the property
- Final wording for the contract will be agreed.

During this period neither buyer nor seller is legally committed to complete the deal. If you receive a higher offer, you are quite at liberty to accept it, taking into consideration the points discussed earlier. Your buyer, too, may find another property he or she prefers. Either of you can withdraw from the deal up to this point.

- When everyone is ready, you will sign your part of the contract and the buyer will sign his
- The 10 per cent deposit paid by your buyer is accepted by your solicitor
- Contracts are exchanged and the matter becomes legally binding
- If your property is not registered with the Land Registry Office, your solicitor will have to provide an abstract of title which is proof of ownership over a period of 15 years or more
- Your solicitor receives the draft transfer deed or conveyance from the buyer's solicitor for approval
- When the final document has been prepared and approved, you will be asked to sign it. This is known as *execution of the deed*

- Your solicitor sends the buyer's solicitor a completion statement
- On *completion*, your solicitor hands over the deeds in exchange for the money
- Your solicitor pays any balance of the monies over to you and you must pay his bill.

12.
THE MOVE

There is a lot of preparation and planning to undertake once contracts have been exchanged and you have a date when you will actually be moving out of your old house and into the new one. It's an exciting time, if a busy one. With careful planning and forethought, everything should run smoothly and there should be no last-minute hiccups, such as mislaying the cat or the buyer arriving with his removal van hours before you have even started to pack!

Buyer's right of access

Officially, the buyer has no right of access to your home until legal completion of the transaction has taken place and the money has been received in exchange for the keys.

Your best course of action is not to allow your buyer to move anything into the property until that time. Many buyers want to arrange for carpet suppliers to measure up for new carpets and to sort out window sizes for curtains and drapes, and you may be quite willing to allow them in to do so. You might even invite the buyer to spend some time with you while you show him or her where stopcocks and meters are, and take the opportunity to come to a mutually acceptable arrangement over the reading of electricity and gas meters and disconnecting the telephone. However, you should not allow any carpets to be fitted or furniture or other belongings to be delivered in advance of the completion day. Storing bits and pieces in your garage may seem as though you are doing your buyer a good turn, but it is not in your best interest to do so.

The same goes for any gas or electrical appliances. Don't allow them to be installed prior to completion. If for some reason there is a very pressing need for the buyer to have items delivered prior to completion, don't agree without consulting your solicitor first.

Remember that you must leave the property with vacant possession, so don't leave odd bits and pieces of your own to be collected after completion day, but make sure you leave everything you agreed to leave in the first place!

Handing over keys

Your solicitor can hand over the keys on completion. However, the easiest way is to hand them over to the buyer yourself. You need to make sure that *official completion* has taken place *before* you pass on the keys.

Check with your solicitor a couple of days in advance to find out what time the money is likely to be received. Often this takes place about noon, but, of course, times can vary depending upon the solicitors involved. Ask your solicitor to ring you as soon as the matter is resolved and *don't* hand over the keys until he does so. Keep a record of his telephone number so that if he should forget to ring you, you can ring him instead!

It is useful to find out the time of completion so that you can gear your packing and removal arrangements to that time and not find yourself still packing bits and bobs when the new owner arrives with a removal van.

Make sure you hand over *all* the keys to the property, including garage keys and internal door and cupboard keys, together with any second copies you have had made. Don't forget to collect keys from relatives and neighbours. It is also helpful for the new occupant if you label each key so that its lock can be clearly identified.

If you have any manufacturers' brochures for the fitted appliances which are to remain in the property, or any other written material which would benefit the new occupier, leave these, too. Instructions for lighting up the central-heating boiler, or how to operate and set the timer are always helpful.

Removal companies

It is much easier to get a removal company to move everything. Most can arrange to do your packing, too, or to deliver packing cases a few days prior to the move, ready for you to pack smaller items.

You will find names and addresses of removal companies in your Yellow Pages or you can obtain a list from the British Association of Removers (see Useful addresses section). Get estimates for the cost of the move and find out what insurance cover they can offer. Conditions of cover do vary and it is wise to ask for a copy of the policy in writing to see exactly what is covered, what conditions apply and what the procedure is for making a claim should it be necessary to do so. There might, for instance, be a time limit beyond which no claim can be made, or claims may only be made if the packing was done by a professional company rather than by yourself.

Although cover can be arranged through the removal company, you can also contact your own insurance company and either extend your existing contents policy to cover the move or take out a separate policy for it. A premium will be required for this and there is no harm in approaching several insurance companies to get quotations and compare the terms and conditions of the policies being offered. Most policies contain a clause expecting you to pay part of any claim made. Find out what this might be and make sure you are not underinsured in relation to the value of your belongings and the cost of replacing damaged, lost or broken items. You may need special cover for valuables, such as paintings, jewellery, stamp collections, etc. It is up to you to check with the insurers to find out what, if any, exclusions might apply to the policy they provide and what additional cover you will need. If you are moving a distance and it is necessary to leave your belongings in the van overnight, make sure your insurance policy covers this, too. In any event, adequate removal insurance is essential.

It is a good idea to label all crates and boxes with a list of their contents and the room to which they should be delivered in your new home. Take special care if you are packing yourself, especially with delicate items, such as glass and china. If crates have been delivered a few days before the move, this gives you plenty of time to do the job properly. Some removal companies will allow you to hold on to the packing-cases for a few days after the move to allow you plenty of time to unpack, but bear in mind that you must have adequate storage space to keep them during this period and until they are collected by the firm. (Remember too that many removal companies will not accept responsibility for any damage to items they did not pack themselves.)

Another advantage of using a professional removal firm is that they are experienced in the business of lifting and packing furniture and belongings in an orderly and safe manner, and have the proper equipment to move difficult or bulky items, such as pianos, washing-machines, etc. They will deliver your marked crates and packing-cases to the rooms designated on your label. If you label your furniture in the same way, this will arrive in the correct room, too.

Charges will depend upon the length of the journey, the amount of furniture to be moved and the time involved. Get several quotations and remember to ask for a copy of any insurance policy the removal company uses.

Preparing to move is a good excuse to have a good clear-out! There is little point in moving furniture or other items your don't want to keep. Local charity shops are always looking for good-quality items of clothing, bric-à-brac or furniture. You might even find a local 'car boot sale' a good place to dispose of some of your unwanted belongings. Second-hand shops are another alternative, or, if the items are unusable (and if we are honest, most homes accumulate a certain amount of unwanted bits and pieces over the years), pack them appropriately and take them to your nearest local authority disposal site.

If you contact your local authority, they will let you know what steps must be taken to arrange for them to collect unwanted goods that are too big for you to handle yourself. The most important thing is not to leave any of your rubbish behind when you leave the property. The new buyer will not be at all impressed if the property is full of your old and unwanted bits and pieces.

Moving yourself

Again, your Yellow Pages will list names of hire companies in your area. On an ordinary driver's licence, you can drive a vehicle up to 7.5 tonnes laden weight. If you don't want to make three or four separate runs, hire the largest van possible and try to get everything in it in one go. Extra journeys take up more time, cover longer distances and consequently cost you more money.

Charges vary. They could be based on a fixed sum per day or week with unlimited mileage, or a smaller sum plus a charge per mile. You will be asked to leave a deposit and to show your driver's licence. Find out what insurance cover is included and what amount you will be expected to pay towards the cost of any damage you might cause to the vehicle. Ask if you can have a trolley for moving heavier things, like the freezer or cooker.

Don't underestimate the length of time you need the van. Check pick-up times and the time the van should be returned. Bear in mind that moving house is an exhausting and time-consuming business and an extra day's hire might give you a little more breathing-space if there has been an unexpected hold-up or a problem you had not expected! Make sure you are properly insured if you have to leave the loaded van overnight.

Collect boxes and suitable packing material well in advance and take special care with breakable objects. Remember that what goes in the van first will come out last, so plan how you are going to load the van before you pick it up. Load up carefully too. It is a traffic offence to overload a vehicle. Load everything firmly so that it can't roll around or move about. Protect furniture with old rugs or blankets so that nothing is scratched or damaged, and try to distribute the weight as evenly as possible. Be careful how you lift and move things. You don't want to damage your back and spend the first few weeks in your new home flat out in bed.

It must be said that moving yourself is very hard work and you will certainly need the help of friends and relatives. Be prepared for a very tiring day with little time for the simple things in life, like eating and drinking, and don't forget to find out what time your buyer will be arriving to move in!

Check-list for preparing your move

- Obtain estimates from removal companies and self-drive van hire companies
- Collect boxes and suitable packing materials
- Find out from your solicitor what time completion is likely to take place
- Collect all the keys of the property and label them ready for your buyer
- Decide whether your solicitor will be handing over the keys or what other arrangements it will be necessary to make

- Contact your buyer and make sure he or she knows where to collect the keys. Make sure you know where to pick up your new ones, too!

- Arrange for final readings of gas and electricity meters

- Contact British Telecom and arrange for your final account to be organised

- Make suitable arrangements for appliances, such as cookers, washing-machines and dishwashers, to be disconnected and, where necessary, reconnected at your new property

- Buy 'change of address' cards and circulate them to all your friends and relatives

- Notify your bank, insurance company, hire-purchase company, credit card company and other personal business contacts of your new address

- Arrange with your local post office to redirect your mail

- Contact your insurance company and arrange for suitable cover for the move

- Make suitable provision for moving pets. Cat baskets can be purchased or hired from your local vet. Boarding kennels need to be booked well in advance to be assured of a place. Remember that moving home is just as traumatic for your pets as it is for you

- You may decide that the children will be more of a hindrance than a help during the move, so prepare baby-sitters and minders well in advance

- Notify the children's school of the intended move and new address. Where a change of school is necessary, make the arrangements well in advance of the move

- When you begin to pack, mark every box and crate with a list of its contents and the room of its destination

- If you are leaving fitted carpets, it is a nice idea to get them cleaned, ready for your buyer

- Arrange for all your rubbish to be removed

- Check that you have left behind everything you agreed with the buyer in the first place

- Cancel your milk and papers and settle up bills

- Leave suppliers' manuals or instructions, etc which might be useful for the buyer
- Muster friends and relatives to help with the move if you are doing it yourself
- Leave the property as clean as you can.

Conclusion

Buying, selling and moving home is often fraught with difficulty and quite exhausting – and most people vow never to do it again! However, statistics prove that the majority of families decide to move home several times, quite apart from moves forced upon them by business or change of circumstances.

Your move will certainly run a lot more smoothly if you are properly organised and in contact with your buyer to arrange for the hand-over of the keys and the time you need to be out by.

The secret of success is preparation, both for the expected *and* the unexpected – like the cat disappearing just as you want to leave, the van being stuck in a traffic jam, or the removal men getting lost on the way!

Try to put some fun in the day. Bear in mind that if the men arrange furniture in the rooms, the ladies will come along and want it all moved somewhere else, even if you originally planned the room layout together!

13.
THE EXPENSES

You will certainly have saved money by selling your home yourself. Estate agents' charges can be between 1 and 3 per cent of the eventual selling price. Property shops and other types of property sellers charge a set amount for taking a property on to their register, whether or not they sell it. Their charges vary, of course. However, as a private seller, your only outlay so far will have been for advertising.

Solicitor's fees will, of course, have to be paid and this is now going to be your most expensive outlay. Charges for carrying out the work vary and, as we have already mentioned, it is important to shop around for comparisons. However, there are certain additional expenses which you will be obliged to pay, especially if you are buying another property. In this chapter we will discuss these charges and what they are for. Also included is some additional information about insurances which you will find useful.

Mortgage redemption charges

You may have to pay your lender an additional amount when you pay off your existing mortgage, if you have one. Although many lenders no longer make a charge, there are still one or two who do, so when you decide the time has come to sell your home, contact your lender and find out how much you currently owe on mortgage and if an addition charge will be made if that mortgage is paid up on completion of your sale. The charge can be as much as three months' additional interest on the advance, although this is often waived if another mortgage is taken out with the same lender. However, it's worth checking to find out where you stand.

Legal charges

There will be a charge made for carrying out the legal work. Some solicitors and conveyancers fix an amount (usually based on the purchase price of the property), while others make a charge dependent upon the amount of work involved.

Other legal expenses include:

- Land registration fees. A buyer must pay the appropriate charges for registration of the new transaction with the Land Registry Office. If the property has already been registered, the charges are lower than for first registration.

- Stamp duty. A buyer must pay stamp duty on his or her purchase if the purchase price is over £30,000. The charge is currently (1988/89) 1 per cent of the total purchase price.

- Search fees. A buyer must pay the appropriate charge for local authority searches made by his or her solicitor.

- Mortgagee's solicitor's fees. A buyer must pay the legal fees for his or her lender's solicitor. If the solicitor acting for the lender happens to be the buyer's solicitor, too, then this charge is usually slightly less.

- Disbursements. These are usually only minor and cover such things as telephone calls and postage, although many solicitors no longer make a separate charge for these.

- VAT on the legal fees.

Building society inspection fee

As we have already discussed, lenders will insist that an inspection is made of the property by a suitably qualified surveyor. The applicant must pay this fee when he or she applies for their mortgage.

Survey fees

A buyer may require a more in-depth survey to be carried out. Fees will depend upon the type of survey chosen.

Removal fees

Either by a professional firm or by doing it yourself. Allow for a deposit if you are hiring a van and for the premium for insurance cover.

Bridging loan

A buyer may require bridging finance in order to complete the purchase or raise the required deposit. Some banks charge an arrangement fee for this. Interest will also have to be paid.

Here is a list of expenses you can use to make a note of your anticipated outgoings:

Advertising costs	£_____
Repayment of existing mortgage	£_____
Mortgage redemption charge (if any)	£_____
Solicitor's charges	£_____
Land registration fee	£_____
Stamp duty	£_____
Search fees	£_____
Disbursements	£_____
Building society inspection fee	£_____
Additional survey fees	£_____
Removal costs	£_____
Interest and charges on bridging finance	£_____
VAT	£_____

A word about insurance

When you move home, there are certain insurances which are essential. If you decide to take out a repayment mortgage, you will need a *mortgage protection insurance*.

All repayment mortgages must be accompanied by a mortgage protection policy. A basic policy will provide enough money to pay off the mortgage in full should the borrower die before the end of the term of the advance. As the outstanding capital is gradually paid off, so the cover decreases, providing just the right amount to cover the mortgage at any one time. Lenders will arrange cover through an insurance company of their choice, but if the borrower wishes to arrange his own cover, the company must be approved by the lender.

Where an endowment mortgage has been obtained, the *endowment policy* is different from the above. The cover provides for the mortgage to be repaid in full if the borrower should die before the end of the mortgage term is reached. If the policy is 'with profits', a lump sum could also be forthcoming, based on the return the insurer has received on his investment of the premiums. When a 'non-profit' policy matures it provides only enough to pay off the mortgage.

Indemnity insurance or mortgage guarantee bond

Extra security is required by lenders when an amount is borrowed which exceeds 75 or 80 per cent of the valuation of the property. This takes the form of a mortgage guarantee bond, or indemnity policy, which the lender arranges with an insurer, who then guarantees the lender against any loss he or she might incur by lending the extra amount. Payment is made by one single premium at the beginning of the term.

Household policy

The sensible home-owner will insure the contents of his or her home from the day they move in. Premiums are based on the value of the items to be insured and a variety of risks are covered, such as theft, fire, flood, riots, explosions, subsidence – even earthquake. The cover provided, terms, conditions and charges vary, so shop around for the best deal and make sure valuables are reassessed on a regular basis and the policy amended accordingly to ensure that adequate cover is always provided. When you move house, contact your insurance company and notify them of the change, so that the policy is dated correctly and you are not left uninsured on the day you move.

Building insurance

Adequate insurance is an essential part of home-ownership. One very important condition the lender will insist upon, before granting a mortgage, is that insurance in the form of a house-building policy is taken out by the borrower.

The policy will cover the cost of rebuilding the property should it be destroyed by a disaster of some kind. In most cases, it is the lender himself who arranges the policy and the cover takes effect from the day contracts are exchanged, when for insurance purposes the buyer becomes responsible for the property. The lender pays the initial premium, which is added to the advance and the repayments amended accordingly. The borrower will be notified of the amount for which the property is to be insured, and the renewal premium will become due once a year. As building costs and property values rise, this insurance should be reviewed annually and, where appropriate, increased to ensure adequate cover is maintained. Many lenders will insist on this anyway and most policies are index-linked. Figures for this type of policy are based on the House Rebuilding Cost Index, which is produced each year by the Royal Institution of Chartered Surveyors (see Useful addresses section).

Conclusion

It is important for all buyers and sellers to budget for their move and to set aside enough money to pay for all the fees and charges associated with moving home.

Hopefully, you will not have been in a position where charges have been incurred, but the deal has fallen through. The problem here, of course, is that all such charges and expenses must be paid, even though the transaction has come to nothing. This is why it is so important to negotiate your sale carefully, doing your best to ensure that you only agree a sale to someone who is unlikely to let you down.

The same applies to any purchase you are making. Here, your first expense will probably be your inspection and survey fees. These do not come cheaply. Therefore before you part with your money, your negotiations to purchase should be on just as strong a foundation as your negotiations to sell.

14.
SELLING A HOUSE
IN SCOTLAND

Selling property in Scotland is slightly different from selling in England and Wales.

It is usual for solicitors to sell property on behalf of their clients. If you want your solicitor to sell for you, there will be a set fee, which is a percentage of the eventual selling price (usually around 1 per cent). Solicitors advertise in solicitors' property centres, where buyers can call in to collect specifications and make viewing appointments through any of the solicitors advertising there. There can be a charge for this type of advertising, but it does give you access to a wide market, as most solicitors advertise the properties they are selling in this way. A property centre is often the first place buyers visit to find out what is available.

There are a few estate agents, too, who sell on a commission basis or, of course, you can sell your property yourself.

If you decide to do this, the first step is to inform your solicitor. He or she will need to prepare certain information and make arrangements for paying off your existing mortgage.

In England, it is usual for solicitors to be informed of the sale once an offer has been received and accepted. The deal does not become legally binding until contracts have been exchanged, which is usually some considerable time later. In Scotland, the system is somewhat different. The contract becomes legally binding as soon as an offer is received and formally accepted, so it is important for your solicitor to prepare the relevant documentation prior to this.

All the offers you receive are best passed on to your solicitor for consideration. This is because in Scotland the buyer can make an offer with certain terms or conditions, and these conditions can have an effect on the acceptability of the offer itself. Your solicitor will then go through each offer and advise you which one is the most suitable to accept. These terms or conditions can cover things such as the date of entry or the furniture and fittings to remain in the property.

Setting a price

In Scotland, it is usual for buyers to make the highest offer they feel appropriate, based on the basic price the seller sets and their surveyor's report. This means you will have to come up with a minimum price. If you then find several interested parties, you can set a closing date by which their sealed bids should be received by your solicitor. Your solicitor will check the terms and conditions of each bid before a decision is made over which one to accept. If you set a basic price, make sure it is adequate to pay off any existing mortgage you may have. Make a list of all the items you intend to leave in the property and any you want to sell separately and be prepared to negotiate on these.

If the property is difficult to sell, the alternative is to set a fixed price. In this case, it is usual for the first offer received for that amount to be accepted, subject to any terms and conditions the buyer puts forward.

Advertising

If you decide to sell yourself, you will need to advertise your property. Make your advertisement as detailed as possible. As we mentioned earlier in the book, it is a good idea to study the layout and content of the advertisements already being used before you decide on your own. You will probably need to be more specific than in England and include a more detailed description of the property. If you know the property is not mortgageable for some reason, you need to make this clear to the reader by stating that the property is only suitable for a cash buyer.

You should also include the address of the property and any special features. Don't forget to sell the *benefits* of your property too – what it is that makes your particular home such a good buy.

Also include the rateable value, room sizes and viewing arrangements. Give telephone numbers of your home and your work. You could also mention times when viewing would be convenient. Also include the name and address of your solicitor, to whom all offers should be made in writing.

Receiving offers

Most people will let you know if they are interested in making an offer as you show them around. In Scotland, though, buyers will need to approach a surveyor to inspect the property on their behalf. Most will base their final offer on the report the surveyor provides, so you must be prepared to let surveyors look around the property whenever this is necessary.

It is not a good idea to accept offers made directly to you. Remember that once an offer has been formally accepted in Scotland, the matter becomes binding, so make sure all offers are directed to your solicitor. If the interested party wants to make an offer, but is waiting upon the report of his surveyor, his solicitor will contact your solicitor to register the interest of his client. If this is the case, you will not be expected to sell to anyone else until the surveyor has called, reported to the prospective buyer and an offer has been made.

Where an offer has been received and the price is acceptable but the terms and conditions are not, your solicitor can go back to the buyer's solicitor and renegotiate the terms of the offer. However, once an offer has been formally accepted, the deal becomes legally binding to both parties. This is called 'missives' in Scotland and is similar to the exchange of contracts in England.

Your solicitor will forward the title of the property to the buyer's solicitor as soon as missives have been concluded. This will be checked by the buyer's solicitor to make sure everything is in order and in the best interests of the buyer. The title is transferred in a deed, called a disposition. You will have to move out on or before the agreed date of entry. On that date, the money will be exchanged for the signed disposition and the keys of the property.

Because you are bound to the contract on acceptance of it, this eliminates the possibility of accepting higher offers at a later date. This, of course, has prevented 'gazumping' taking place in Scotland, but on occasions it forces buyers to make higher offers than perhaps the property is worth, which is good for the seller, but not for the buyer.

As a seller, you also run the risk of having to accept an offer with an agreed date of entry before you have found somewhere else to move to. Therefore, it is important to organise your move carefully and to make arrangements for bridging finance, should it become necessary.

15.
TURNING TO THE
PROFESSIONALS

Of course, there will always be some people who do not wish to tackle the business of selling their property themselves. If you have moved away from the area, leaving the property empty, or are elderly or infirm, you may consider that the services of a professional estate agent are what you need.

Make sure you choose a good agent, though. Listen to neighbours and friends and ask for recommendations. There are good and bad estate agents, but an agent who is a member of the National Association of Estate Agents (see Useful addresses section) can usually be relied upon.

An agent will prepare specifications and advertise your home for you. Check local newspapers and ask the agent to let you know when each advertisement is placed. A good agent will accompany all viewers who call and will not expect you to show people around. He will find a buyer who is in a good position to complete and will not conclude a deal to anyone who is unlikely to get a mortgage, or who still has a property on the market. He will arrange a mortgage for your buyer if this is necessary, notify solicitors of the deal and monitor it closely as it progresses in order to ensure that a speedy and satisfactory completion is reached. He will report to you on a regular basis to keep you fully informed of what is going on, and will provide a For Sale board if you want one.

Estate agents' fees range from 1 to 3 per cent of the selling price – which is a lot of money – so you want to make sure you get the best service! These charges must be confirmed to you in writing by the agent under the terms of the Estate Agents Act 1979. As you will be expecting to receive the best possible service, it is a good idea to ask for written confirmation of everything the agent purposes to do to secure a sale for you. If he doesn't meet that obligation, then don't pay up and remember that most agents' fee structure is based on 'no sale, no fee'. A lower fee is usually charged if you instruct the agent on a 'sole agency' basis. This means he is the only agent acting for you. If you decide to instruct an agent on this basis, remember that you can change your mind if the service you receive is not good enough, but if you later instruct other agents, the fee will revert to the norm.

Don't give an agent 'sole selling rights'. Under these terms the agent can claim his commission when the sale is complete, whether or not he was actively involved in the sale himself; which means if you sold privately, you would still have to pay the agent.

Whatever agent you instruct, under whatever terms, the service you receive must be the best. Demand an explanation if you don't hear anything for days on end, or if the agent fails to keep in touch with you. It's your money – don't part with it unless you have received good value for it!

Key reference guide to selling your house

1. Decide upon a realistic marketing price. Compare prices of property similar to your own and in your near neighbourhood. Take into account the age and condition of your home, together with any 'extras' you intend to include in the price. Also decide what is the lowest figure you could possibly accept if you have to consider offers.

2. Make a list of the fixtures and fittings you intend to include in the asking price, and a separate list of any items you want to sell. Decide what price you want for each.

3. Carry out any essential maintenance to your home. If there is a lot of work outstanding and you don't intend to do it before the sale, make sure this is reflected in the price.

4. Consider all the questions a potential buyer is likely to ask and make sure you have all the answers. Make a note of yearly running costs – gas, electricity, etc.

5. Decide what are the best selling points about your home and what the buyer will gain from buying it rather than another property. Bear this in mind as you show people around – make it a 'selling point'.

6. Decide how and where to advertise and prepare a For Sale sign if you want one.

7. Draw up several advertisements before you decide which is the best. If there is little response, analyse exactly why (see Chapter 6). Remember that all property will sell if it is correctly priced, so never give up!

8. Produce written details of the property, to include room sizes, with the emphasis on any special features.

9. Arm yourself with a notebook in which to keep a record of the name, address and telephone number of everyone who

enquires about the sale. This can also be used to record the times of viewing appointments.

10. Don't let people in unless you know who they are!

11. Make sure you are not in the house alone when people call.

12. Present your home at its very best.

13. Try to establish a definite commitment from your viewer before he or she leaves.

14. Hold out for the highest price you can.

15. Only accept an offer from a buyer who is in the best possible position to complete the sale. If in doubt, *keep offering*!

16. When you receive an acceptable offer from an acceptable buyer, complete the check-list included in Chapter 8 and forward it to your solicitor.

17. Send a letter of confirmation to your buyer, too. Make sure all written correspondence is clearly marked 'Subject to Contract and Survey'.

18. If you take a deposit, provide a signed and dated receipt. Pass the deposit on to your solicitor as 'stakeholder'.

19. Monitor the progress of your sale carefully. If any doubts arise, put your home on the market again.

20. Make sure any purchase you are making co-ordinates with your sale.

21. As soon as contracts have been exchanged, prepare for the move. Remember, you must leave behind the fixtures and fittings you agreed when you first negotiated the sale.

22. Remember that your buyer has no right of access unless special arrangements have been made through your solicitor.

23. On the day of completion, make sure the buyer knows where to collect the keys.

24. Now you can relax!

Glossary of legal terms

It is not always easy to understand some of the legal jargon used in the process of buying and selling property; the following list has been provided to shed some light on the subject.

Advance The loan, sometimes called the capital sum or principal sum.
Annuity mortgage A repayment mortgage.
Banker's draft A cheque which is issued by a bank.
Bridging loan A loan made to a buyer to enable him or her to complete their purchase, or for the deposit required when contracts are exchanged.
Completion The final part of the transaction, when the money is paid over in exchange for the title deeds.
Completion statement An account of the amount the buyer must pay on completion of the transaction.
Contract An agreement between the buyer and the seller.
Conveyance A document which transfers the ownership of a property with an unregistered title from the seller to the buyer.
Conveyancing The term traditionally used for the legal side of buying and selling property.
Draft contract The wording suggested for the contract. It can be amended several times before the final wording is agreed and accepted.
Draft transfer The wording suggested for the transfer document.
Easements The rights of way across a property.
Endowment mortgage A loan on which only the interest is paid throughout the term, and which is paid off in a lump sum when the endowment policy matures.
Freehold A property owned absolutely.
Good root Proof of ownership.
Ground rent The amount paid for a lease, usually each year.
Joint tenants Co-ownership of property, where ownership is passed to the survivor on the death of the other partner.
Land registry A government department recording details of property with registered title.
Legal charge A mortgage.
Mortgage A loan for which the property is security.

Mortgagee A lender.

Mortgagor A borrower.

Mortgage protection policy The life insurance required by the buyer to cover the outstanding amount of the loan in the event of his/her death.

Positive covenant Something which must be carried out on or to a property or its land.

Preliminary enquiries The enquiries a solicitor makes about the property and its land before the contract is drawn up.

Purchaser The person or persons buying a property.

Redemption Paying off a loan.

Registered land Land the title of which is registered with HM Land Registry and whose legal ownership is guaranteed by the State.

Repayment mortgage A loan on which part capital and interest is paid throughout the term of the advance.

Restrictive covenant Something which must not be carried out on or to a property or its land.

Stamp duty The tax on certain legal documents.

Subject to contract A period after a sale has been agreed during which either party can withdraw from the deal without penalty.

Tenancy in common Co-ownership of property, where the share in the property can be passed on to anyone of the owner's choice in the event of his/her death.

Title deeds The documents proving ownership of unregistered property of land.

Transfer The document which transfers ownership of property with a registered title from buyer to seller.

Vendor A person selling a property.

Useful addresses

British Association of
  Removers
279 Grays Inn Road
London WC1X 8SY

Council for Licensed
  Conveyancers
Golden Cross House
9 Duncannon Street
London EC2N 4JF
(01) 210 4603

HM Land Registry
32 Lincoln's Inn Fields
London WC2A 3PH
(01) 405 3488

Incorporated Society of Valuers
  and Auctioneers
3 Cadogan Gate
London SW1X 0AS
(01) 235 2282

Law Society of Scotland
PO Box 75
26 Drumsheugh Gardens
Edinburgh EH3 7YR
(031) 226 7411

Building Societies Association
3 Savile Row
London W1X 1AF
(01) 437 0655

Financial Intermediaries',
  Managers' and Brokers'
  Regulators Association
22 Great Tower Street
London EC3R 0HU
(01) 283 4814

Historic Buildings Bureau
2–16 Church Road
Stanmore
Middlesex HA7 4AW

Law Society
113 Chancery Lane
London WC2A 1PL
(01) 242 1222

National Association of
  Estate Agents
Arbon House
21 Jury Street
Warwick CV34 4EH
(0926) 496800

Be your own estate agent

Royal Institution of Chartered Surveyors
12 Great George Street
Parliament Square
London SW1P 3AD
(01) 222 7000

Index